A YOUTH WASTED CLIMBING

A Youth Wasted Climbing

By David Chaundy-Smart

Foreword by John Kaandorp

RMB

Rocky Mountain Books
www.rmbooks.com

Library and Archives Canada Cataloguing in Publication

Smart, David, 1962-, author
     A youth wasted climbing / by David Chaundy-Smart ; foreword by John Kaandorp.

Issued in print and electronic formats.
ISBN 978-1-77160-067-5 (paperback).—ISBN 978-1-77160-068-2 (epub).—ISBN 978-1-77160-069-9 (pdf)

     1. Smart, David, 1962- —Childhood and youth. 2. Mountaineers—Ontario—Biography. I. Title.

GV199.92.S63A3 2015   796.522092   C2015-902007-7
                                                 C2015-902008-5

Typeset by Roseander Main

Front cover photo: Me wearing only my Whillans harness and army surplus sleeping bag from Hercules Surplus in Toronto, on Guano Ledge, West Face of Leaning Tower, Yosemite, 1980. (Brian Hibbert)

Printed in Canada

Rocky Mountain Books acknowledges the financial support for its publishing program from the Government of Canada through the Canada Book Fund (CBF) and the Canada Council for the Arts, and from the province of British Columbia through the British Columbia Arts Council and the Book Publishing Tax Credit.

 Canadian Patrimoine
Heritage canadien

 Canada Council Conseil des Arts
for the Arts du Canada

 BRITISH COLUMBIA
ARTS COUNCIL
Supported by the Province of British Columbia

This book was produced using FSC®-certified, acid-free paper, processed chlorine free and printed with vegetable-based inks.

In memory of Ceretha McKenzie, 1961–2012

What the aristocrat writers get for free from nature, intellectuals of lower birth have to pay for with their youth. Write a story of how a young man ... brought up to respect rank, to kiss priests' hands, and worship the thoughts of others, thankful for every piece of bread, whipped time and again, having to go to lessons in galoshes, brawling, torturing animals, loving to eat at rich relatives' houses, needlessly hypocritical before God and man, merely from a sense of his own insignificance – write a story about how this young man squeezes the serf out of himself, drop by drop, and how waking up one bright morning this young man feels that in his veins there no longer flows the blood of a slave, but the blood of a real man.

—*Anton Chekhov*
A Letter to A.S. Suvorov, January 7, 1889

Reg Smart climbing Smegma Spasmodic Frog in the
Farflung Islets of Langerhans, Rattlesnake Point, 1979.
(Reg Smart III Collection)

Contents

A Foolish and Dangerous Pastime

On a planet bursting with worn-out widgets and increasingly uniform experiences, clambering up hard rock, loose stone and brittle ice remains an essentially misunderstood, exotic and intensely unique experience. When indulged in properly, serious climbing amounts to a tremendous waste of resources, potential and time. It has no economic value for its participants, and under the right circumstances, it remains a foolish and dangerous pastime that consolidates friendships and ends marriages. Naturally, those attributes are part of its appeal.

As a pursuit and pathology, climbing has always been ill-suited to those with an excess of confidence and a dearth of imagination. For those thus equipped, there has always been tamer fare: golf, tennis and bowling come to mind. Climbing continues to be a game without clubs and racquets, and appeals to those those lacking the ambition to acquire these simple tools. Instead, climbing is a complex choice and as such is a pastime littered with its share of misguided dilettantes, photogenic heroes and charismatic madmen. Never really knowing which one of these three you may be tied to while ascending steep ground on a cliff or mountain wall is part of the attraction as well.

David Chaundy-Smart, author of *A Youth Wasted Climbing*, was both at the core and forefront of a small and talented fraternity of climbers that emerged from suburban Ontario high schools in the mid-to-late 1970s. Under the uniform grey of the classroom and the rigidity of the school system, they emerged from their schools underwhelmed, undistinguished and dissatisfied. With little equipment and less experience, but increasing boldness, they picked up the almost dormant scent of the corduroy-clad European climbers still clinging to the limestone of the largely unexplored Niagara Escarpment. The trail of rusting, soft steel pitons left on cliffs by these postwar climbers, coupled later with a strong American influence via Yosemite, was somehow the right classroom for budding anarchists like David and his peers, who immediately became hooked by the pleasures and perils of the climbing life. Even today, I gaze at some of David's routes, with their primitive bolts and rusting, oversized bong pitons and wonder how anyone could climb limestone so conspicuously absent of features.

When I hesitantly began climbing in the winter of 1979 on the overburnished limestone cliffs of Rattlesnake Point in Ontario, I already knew of David by reputation. If memory serves, when I first met David, I was teetering up some thin and slippery face climb on the sharp end of the rope, when he suddenly appeared beside me and offered words of encouragement. What struck me were his youthfulness, his kindness and the fact that he was climbing without a rope.

I made that climb that day, and many others since, but I climbed better for having met him. I suspect many others have as well.

Later, as I grew into the wider climbing community establishing itself in southern Ontario, I was in awe of his talent, vision and equipoise on steep rock. But these things also irritated me. David brought to his climbing a carefully groomed aura of invincibility and confidence that created a certain buzz or magic around his exploits that I seemingly couldn't participate in. Fortunately, as I matured, the petty and self-inflicted irritations of youth grew into something more substantial and positive. I allowed myself to be influenced by David's passion and boldness as a climber and his enthusiasm as an archivist as we stumbled, largely independent of one another, through the chaos of our formative years.

I suspect that for David the exercise of writing about climbing is similar to ascending a familiar route of one's own creation, in the sense that everything is knowable and graspable: the cracks, bumps and positive edges that provide holds; the nuances of texture that provide friction; and the sequences of movement or tricks necessary to unlock the puzzle of the route.

But not so memoir. It seems to me that the act of writing an intensely personal history of the challenges of youth, with all its opportunities and obstacles, is more like descending a long, difficult and largely unfamiliar route, without the benefits of a rope and a reliable partner muttering encouraging things from the other end. If the point of climbing down a route is to arrive at the bottom of the cliff, then perhaps the point of memoir is to arrive at the bottom of one's experience through the long journey of writing alone. Staring at a blank sheet of paper or stone may amount to the same problem: What can I do with this? Why am I choosing to do this? Where will I arrive, and with what new insights?

I enjoy the idea of David the memoirist sounding his personal history on the way down a wall of words he has built, in the same way that competent climbers test holds on the way up, tapping the stone with either piton hammers or bruised knuckles, acutely listening for the creaks and hollowness that betray specious holds. At the very least, struggling with a memoir is an adventure into descending through the vapours of memory, and an attempt not only to take hold of the ethereal information that is or was there, but of what one thought and hoped was there. Memory can be as suspect as loose rock.

Serious writing and climbing are both perilous journeys. Writers and climbers share the pleasures of distraction, the necessity of intense focus and a necessary suspension of the need to know exactly what one is reaching for. Both are filled with beauty, grace, terror and profound joy. David, through *A Youth Wasted Climbing*, has masterfully and modestly reminded the climber and reader within each of us of these powerful elements.

—*John Kaandorp*
Allenford, Ontario

Acknowledgements

During the years of working on this book, I was helped by many people in many ways, but I wish to first thank those whose stories are mixed up with my own. For the sake of an author who in many cases was a mere acquaintance from the past, they remembered and sometimes researched what might have seemed trivial, rightfully forgotten or just as rightfully kept to themselves. Any pleasure or insight that can be derived from these pages is as much the product of their lives and voices as it is my own. Any shortcomings in the book, however, are wholly mine.

I am indebted to many friends and colleagues for special assistance. John Harlin III; Paul Pritchard; Chic Scott; my brother, Reg Smart; my father, Reginald Smart II; Tom Valis; Ed Webster; and my wife, Rosalind Chaundy, read drafts and offered many useful suggestions to improve them. Peter Arbic, Gerry Banning, Geoff Creighton, Steve De Maio, William Jack, John Kaandorp, Richard Massiah, Jamie Paddon,

Chris Rogers, Rob Rohn, Mike Tschipper, Tom Valis and many others helped remember things. The staff at Roseander Main, Gripped Publishing's art house, and especially Warren Wheeler and James Cook, have, as always, gone beyond their duties in art and design to offer invaluable editorial advice. Jim Mark, of course, inspired many of the events in this book by writing *Rock Climbing in Ontario* in 1974. Without my parents, Reg and Lillian Smart, I would never have had many of the experiences I describe in this book, and I thank them for their support. A few names, places and events have been changed because of failures of memory.

CHAPTER 1

The Farm on the Hill

Eyes glinted in the shadows of abandoned filing cabinets and desks. The door creaked behind us. My heart was beating quickly, but I had to see what was in the darkness. Although Reg knew things like this could work out badly from reading *Tales from the Crypt* comics, he was even more curious. We froze until our eyes adjusted to the light and made out a ventriloquist's dummy with grinning lips and glass eyes. Laughing so hard we were short of breath, we ran down the stairs and told the old man what we had found.

Granddad leaned across the paper-cutting machine and shouted, "Hell if I'd go in there," above the pounding of the machines, even though he had dared us to.

My brother, Reg, and I looked forward to the times when my mother left us in Granddad's printing shop so she could go on errands. It was in the Junction, an old neighbourhood in the west end of Toronto that was home to slaughterhouses, rail yards, prostitutes and criminals. The shop was an ink-stained basement cave where machines crashed below flickering light bulbs and the air was thick with the smells of machine oil and lead from movable type.

Granddad had been to darker places than the room up the stairs. Years of drinking ended the night he was brought home drunk from the Shoemakers' Club, a printers' bar, by a female dwarf. My grandmother, whose only vices were chain-smoking and my Granddad, lost patience. She insisted he sober up immediately, and he never drank again.

She seemed, however, not to object to his lifelong gambling habit. He kept a roll of bills handy to peel off for the craps games and for bookies who took bets on horses or wrestlers with handles like Strangler, Whipper, Killer and Bronco. In the bouts in downtown arenas there were no costumes, and the injuries were real. Losers in Loser Leaves Town matches really had to leave town. The fighters were so tough that Granddad once bet on a light-bulb-eating contest between two wrestlers.

Granddad remembered the bad days before the Second World War, when he worked at Canada Packers. His job was shooting penned cows in the head with a short-barrelled rifle. He had scores of stories about easy money, hard money, shady mining deals, the Great Depression and how he surprised even himself by landing in the middle class.

Although he was a made man in the Junction, Granddad had critics in his family. My Uncle Bud had married Granddad's shy sister, Mary, who proved suited to her husband's sometimes clandestine world. Bud started out as a US customs officer on the Panama Canal and then worked for the Secret Service in Africa during the Second World War. He claimed to know all the best nightclubs and restaurants from Cape Town to Cairo. When the war ended, he had bad nerves and spent two years on a cruise ship, looking over his shoulder to see if he was being followed. When he felt the threat had passed, he settled his family in an apartment in New York City. He appeared to be unemployed, despite his swell lifestyle.

Every day he breakfasted in his dining room decorated with Chinese paintings, put on a double-breasted suit and a tie and walked to the Metropolitan Museum of Art. If any pictures had been moved, he complained to the curator. Afterwards, he sat in Central Park, reading the paper. This idyll continued for years until someone kicked him in the shin while he read. It was just a bruise, but Bud decided that New York had become dangerous and moved to a similar apartment on Avenue Road in downtown Toronto, near the Royal Ontario Museum.

Granddad's sister had made few demands on Bud, but now that she was back in her hometown, she wanted to have dinner parties with her family. Bud tried to get Mary to just invite the one or two relatives he hated the least for the less-committing dessert and coffee, but she made him attend large family gatherings at my grandfather's house.

On one occasion, Granddad put out a full bottle of rye whisky and a shot glass decorated with cowboys on broncos and told Bud there was no more liquor in the house. Bud drained the bottle and asked for more. Granddad tried to ignore him by watching the golf game on his living room television set. It was one of the first colour sets, and the grass was a hypnotic bright green. Bud didn't give up easily. He asked if Granddad saw the white ball go in the hole or if he thought they'd lost it. Then he would talk about the opera season and offer to buy Granddad tickets if he was short of dough.

Granddad stopped pretending to ignore Bud only when it was time for him to leave. Aunt Mary seemed not to notice that Bud had spent the evening insulting her brother. She smiled as she helped her family man stagger into the cockpit of his European convertible. My grandfather, who had worked hard for his Oldsmobile cars and homburgs, could no longer resist asking Bud how he made a living.

Leaning over the windshield, Bud checked back and forth and said in a low voice, "As a young man, Reg, I invested in kewpie dolls. Kewpie dolls are the way of the future." Then he reversed onto Burnhamthorpe Road at high speed without checking his rear-view mirror.

Bud's wealth and high-class cultural tastes galled my

grandfather, but not as much as his own children's disloyalty against the printing trade and their belief that their father was a philistine. The conflict between generations was led by Granddad's first-born son and namesake, who would later become my father.

Reg Junior was no rebel, although as a young man, he had briefly flirted with adventure. After reading *Beau Geste*, he and a friend placed an advertisement in a magazine offering themselves as mercenaries, with the caveat that they were unwilling to break the law. They received no job offers. He got a driver's licence as soon as he could and had a brief spell as a hot-rodder. He was, however, better known for his love of school, poetry, novels, art galleries and listening to classical music on the radio. Accepted after high school into the University of Toronto, he dated girls who had been to private schools, and he wore a college blazer into his thirties. He excelled in psychology, a new academic discipline at the university.

These tastes and interests annoyed my grandfather, who preferred boxing matches and pictures of dogs playing cards. While my father was just the first of his siblings to choose books over the printing press, he was blamed for starting the rebellion. Family life was a struggle before he met his most powerful ally: my future mother, Lillian.

Lillian grew up behind the municipal abattoir on Niagara Street in Toronto. Her father was a gardener for the City of Toronto who painted watercolours in his spare time. He enlisted in the army in 1918, but just as his unit was about to ship for England from Montreal, the officers discovered that he was too young, and he was sent home. He died on Christmas Day, 1945, when Lillian was ten. Incredibly, by my time, no could seem to remember the cause of death. Lillian, her younger sister, Joan, and her brother, Ron, a polio survivor, were supported by what their mother, Lillian Senior, made at a biscuit factory. Lillian Senior's father, Walter, and his brother, Arthur, became the men of the family.

Walter, Arthur and Lillian Senior were born outside the army base in Shoeburyness, on England's Essex coast, a few years after the town was invaded by Martians in H.G. Wells's *The War of the Worlds*. They immigrated to Toronto before the First World War. Within days of the outbreak of the war, Walter and Art queued up at Fort York to enlist with the First Canadian Contingent. The Fijian tattoos Arthur had acquired in the navy were recorded by the recruiting sergeant to help identify his corpse in case his head was blown off. Walter wrote "knows firearms" on his attestation papers, although he also ticked the space beside "no military experience." The sergeant helping him with the form described a tattoo of a flaming Union Jack nailed to a crucifix on his right bicep. A day after arriving in England, Walter went absent without leave for a week.

The army docked his pay and put him in the field artillery.

He spent the next four years lobbing poison gas shells at the Germans from colossal trench mortars. Twice in hospital for lungs ravaged by mustard gas and three times for the clap, he returned to Toronto a year after the shooting stopped. He brought back a British War Medal embossed with Saint George trampling a Prussian shield in a bone-strewn no man's land, and the Victory Medal, engraved "The Great War to Save Civilization." I still have them.

Having saved civilization, Walter retired to a place on Niagara Street, drew veterans' benefits, gambled in the park and caroused at the Legion Hall. (Arthur had served in the artillery supply train and was unscathed, so he took a travelling job with the railways.) Walter tried to help with his grandchildren, but serving the Empire made him an old man by his forties, and old men could not be expected to change their ways.

On Sundays, when the bars were closed, veterans gambled in the park. When the cops sauntered by, Walter and his comrades threw their money and dice over a hedge. Since swings were chained up to prevent children having fun on the Lord's Day, Lillian and her best friend, Dorcas, were available to scramble under the hedges after the dice and cash, in exchange for nickels.

Walter and Arthur died before I was born, and I only remember Lillian Senior as she was decades later: a gaunt hunchback with an acrid Macdonald cigarette in her lips, her mug of builder's tea guarded by a bony growling chihuahua that one of my cousins described as more of a voodoo doll than a dog. Her accent blended the soft tones of the Thames Estuary with nasal, working-class Canadian, but she spoke little, perhaps guarding memories, perhaps hardened to silence by the years of work and scarcity.

My mother's sister, Joan, always kept dogs and cats, but over the years she also had canaries, mynas, skunks, rats, monkeys, ferrets and squirrels. She married an alcoholic – a veterinarian's assistant who lived in an animal hospital – but left him when he had twins with another woman. Joan spent years shuttling my cousin, Wayne, and his sisters from apartment to apartment, frequently after evictions. One move to a no-pets-allowed apartment meant that young Wayne had to help her kill most of her menagerie with stolen sodium pentothal. Joan lived on social assistance, and besides the animals, which were sometimes so numerous that her children went hungry to feed them, her hobby was a dire cigarette addiction.

Wayne escaped to outer space. In the midst of a gloomy public housing project, he built a world based on comic books, movies and spacecraft. Adults cringed at his erotically tinged, science-fiction drawings, but they were the basis of a materially unrewarding but prolific career that won him the respect of other fans. Eventually he began answering only to the name Taral, which came from a language he invented; my mother called it his "spaceman name." Taral was ten years older than me, so we were never really friends, but I looked up to him as the first person I knew who lived by the authority of his imagination. My mother, however, disapproved of Taral and outer space in general. She understood the need to escape, she just saw it in more terrestrial, material terms.

In fact, although my mother and father were named after their parents, neither of them wanted to live as they had been raised. This desire was one of the things that brought them together to create the suburban family life I knew. Lillian dropped out of high school to work as a secretary at Tip Top Tailors' art deco head office on Lake Shore Boulevard. Naturally charming, skinny from a tough childhood and attractive despite it, she made friends easily. Her challenge was figuring out how to use what providence had given her in lieu of money or education to escape her limited world. If she needed a reminder of the perils of marrying within her class, she need only remember her unfortunate sister.

The church at the nearby army barracks was the only place outside of the office where she might meet middle-class men her age. No matter how graceful and well-dressed she was, however, they knew she was working class. But just a streetcar ride north, there were wealthy parishes where people could only judge her by her clothes, which she made in the latest style on her sewing machine, and middle-class manners, which she could learn.

Interning at a mental hospital as a graduate student,

my father was compelled to play Santa Claus at the patients' Christmas party. There, he met my mother –she was the leader of a team of elves (actually parishioners from her church) bringing gifts they had donated.

They dated for a year and then married. Etobicoke, a new suburb of low-density cookie-cutter housing with parks, shopping malls and modern schools, was irresistible and affordable. New wealth and mass production meant a suburbanite couple could buy a house, a swimming pool, appliances and a car. These were essential because the subway wasn't extended to Etobicoke until several years after my parents bought their home. Their house was more than a mile from the last stop, and the nearest shopping malls were about as far. The term *homemaker* was synonymous with *wife*, and my mother stayed home. Their first child, Reg, was born on Halloween in 1960. I was their second, born on the last day of September 1962.

My memories of being outdoors begin five years later, in the creek beds, ravines and woodlots of Etobicoke, which were beginning to disappear under concrete and tarmac. Reg, a handful of other neighbourhood boys and I built deadfall forts and skirmished like our tv heroes on *Combat!* and *Hawkeye and the Last of Mohicans*. On television, gis and frontiersmen might lower their weapons, but they rarely put them down. Armed with realistic plastic copies of the weapons we saw on tv (scaled down for children's hands), we spent hours outdoors re-enacting battles. The history we learned at school validated TV, portraying Canada's past as a series of epic camping trips and shootouts in the forest. Like most boys of the 1960s, we played outside because that was where the Wild West and the Second World War happened, not because we wanted to commune with nature.

M y parents weren't hippies, but their growing affluence let them indulge a longing for nature that would prove fateful for my brother and me. They had two daughters and two sons now and wanted a weekend property where they could set us loose while they relaxed. A cottage in Muskoka would have been more prestigious, but a farm was affordably in tune with the craze for pioneer-style furniture and Gordon Lightfoot's folk music. In 1969 my father paid $6,000 for a disused two-hundred-acre farm two hours' drive north of the city, on the Niagara Escarpment, a limestone ridge stretching from Manitoulin Island to Niagara Falls. McGillivray's Hill sat between the walled gorge of Devil's Glen and meadows and forests sloping down the escarpment to Glen Huron.

As a city child, I delighted in the broad fields and woods the farm added to my world. In summer, grasshoppers leapt clicking in feral hay. Roads of crushed stone from the long-forsaken kiln billowed white behind the occasional passing car. From the crest of the hill you could see the harbour town of Collingwood on the verge of the turquoise Georgian Bay.

The woods edged the escarpment cliffs. Tiny grey barns dotted distant pastures and fields below.

My father sometimes sat in the road on top of the hill with a box of oil paints, trying to render the scene with colours right out of the tubes: the bay cobalt blue, the fields malachite green, the sky cerulean blue. One of those simple yet moving little paintings hangs in my home. It reminds me that learning that hill's natural palette of sounds, colours and smells was, perhaps, the best part of my childhood.

The first farmers had gathered the fieldstones into barrows where snakes and groundhogs now lived. Between the fields were hedgerows where birch and scrub maple burst apart skeletal rail fences. A few fields were harvested for forage once a year, but most of the land was fallow. Burdock and milkweed rose between the groves of twisted fruit trees where, in the fall, we picked sour apples once grown for the pigs. Beyond the old orchards were the dark green acres of forest where deer browsed in drifts of white trillium and silver beeches rose like pillars from the undergrowth.

The hill's white rock erupted from a thin layer of moss. Lined with grasses, the clifftop game trail swerved between stones as big as cars. Sometimes, if you lay on the cliff edge and looked down, a black vulture dropped from a ledge, spreading ragged wings as far across as a man is tall. Slowly, it would beat the clear air, its naked red head looking backwards as it barely hurdled the treetops. After Reg told me the vultures only ate dead things, I lay like a corpse on the trail to see if one would land. As soon as I saw a circling bird, I ran away.

Below the cliffs, dark gullies filled with talus blocks, and wet logs formed mazes dripping with sawtoothed ferns. The farm had no pond, and hot days made us brave enough to clamber down to feel the cold air flowing from below the rocks. If Reg heard a porcupine scratch, he teased me by saying it was a bear, but it took more courage to run away by myself than it did to stay with him.

One sweltering day, we discovered a pinnacle proud of the face carved a hundred years before with inscriptions like: anglo-saxon countrys owe prosprity to the protestnt faith of our ancesters. Whatever the words meant, seeing them gave me a chill, for I knew that all that was left of the author's world was my playground of ruined fields, collapsed barns and rusted tractors. Years later, when I climbed the route of a dead man I had known, I felt something similar.

At the farm we learned the power of real weapons. I still have scars from my knife collection, which included a wicked six-inch folding blade, a Swiss army knife, a fixed-blade hunting knife I found in a field and a bayonet for a Lee-Enfield rifle that I was only allowed to handle under my father's supervision. Reg and my father were constantly strafing groundhogs, trees and fence posts with their air rifle, .22-calibre rifle and 20-gauge shotgun, all of which my father had bought from the glass case at the Canadian Tire store.

They were great shots. Once, with the car packed and everyone ready to go, my father saw a groundhog standing on a rock on the cliff edge. He steadied the rifle on the car door, it cracked and the animal disappeared. We ran to the cliff and found only a trickle of blood.

The war on groundhogs was, however, usually bloodless. Following the advice of a friend of my father who had combat experience, we lit fires in their burrow holes to smoke them out. They just escaped unseen out other holes, and Reg ended up shooting into the smoking dirt. We gave up the tactic after the wind blew the flames out of a hole into a day-long grassfire. When we returned two weeks later, acres of hilltop were black stubble. A couple of vultures circled in the sky above the smoking molar root of charred fieldstones.

Reg spent his days wandering the fields and woodlots, hoping for a rabbit but usually just studding fence posts with lead pellets. I was happy exploring the trails along the cliffside alone, playing in the barn or pretending to drive the wrecked tractors and cars that sat rusting close by.

Unfortunately for Reg and me, McGillivray's Hill was not a paradise for our parents. The roads became rivers after storms, and my mother had to cook without running water or electricity. My sisters, who were still quite small, had no interest in rifles and trails. If they left the farmhouse, they tripped on rocks, lost boots in the mud or were bitten by insects. My mother had lived without amenities as a child and worked hard to get them. For her, the charms of the lime-stone countryside didn't offset the chore of a weekend without modern conveniences.

It didn't take long for my father's infatuation with rural life to wane. "Nature," he later wrote, reflecting on his time at McGillivray's Hill, "never seemed neutral or benign, but always enraged and anti-human." Hyperbole aside, I believe the outdoors simply didn't offer him as much pleasure as books, tennis or listening to classical music on his stereo. He was just more at home in brown shoes and a blazer than work clothes and rubber boots. When burglars broke in and stole some antique furniture, my mother convinced him to put the place up for sale. She personally auctioned it off from the farmhouse's front porch.

I saw the farm for what I believed would be the last time out the rear window of the family car in late summer 1972. A veil of road dust rose as we went over McGillivray's Hill, and it was gone. Reg was sad and angry. The three years he had spent there had made it an irreplaceable home for him. My quietness hid inner turmoil. My childish belief that destiny would respect my feelings and memories and one day bring me back revealed a romantic weakness that would shape my life. It was the first place to seduce me. I later found out that not everyone is vulnerable to places in this way, but it is a weakness I shared with many climbers.

When we were young men, Reg went back to see if the

place had changed. The locked and shuttered house was still an Andrew Wyeth study in red brick and grey wood. Below the old trails, he found a cliff scoured clean by a paleolithic glacier. He climbed a beautiful, knife-thin crack up the centre of the wall. I met him there after driving across a field to camp by the cliffside. In the middle of the cold night I sat up, aware of lights outside. Beyond the white crescent of Collingwood, a few boat lights sparked in the dark bay, and the sky was full of meteors. I watched them fade and went back to sleep.

The farm sold, and my parents never heard the call of the outdoors again. For a while we lived in England, where my father, now an authority in his profession, took a temporary posting. My parents loved Great Britain and toured sites from Edinburgh Castle to Stonehenge. English school, however, provided a harsher experience of my grandmother's country than the cathedral tour. I hated wearing shorts in the damp winter, the pressure to speak with Received Pronunciation and the disgusting school lunches with nicknames like Dead Man's Leg and Accident in the Alps.

I did, however, like the British obsession with the past, when Britons felt everything had been rationed, glorious and important. I already spent a lot of time daydreaming about improbable or heroic things like the Middle Ages, the French Foreign Legion and space travel, and I was a quick convert to the British fascination with the World Wars.

In Canada there were a few war comics and war programs

on television, but in Britain kids' versions of the Second World War were everywhere. Every week *War Picture Library*, *The Victor* comics and *Commando Comics* published war stories for boys in which principled upper-class officers and working-class Tommies overcame class strife to fight for sportsmanship, decency and Britishness. Outnumbered, they prevailed against hordes of Nazis shouting *"Sieg heil!"* and Japanese soldiers with samurai swords, spectacles and buckteeth whose vocabulary was limited to *"Banzai!"* Time left over from reading about the war was spent building plastic models of its vehicles and aircraft. There were also war movies. While older kids went to rock concerts and protested against war, my generation watched Clint Eastwood and David Niven gunning down Nazis who spoke, even to each other, in badly accented English.

War movies often included technical climbing. In *The Guns of Navarone*, released in 1961 but still in theatres a decade later, commandos climbed a cliff in the Aegean Sea to assault Nazi shore guns. *Raid on Rommel*, from 1971, recycled the plot. In *Where Eagles Dare*, from 1968, the commandos attacked an alpine base and carried the ropes and ice axes they used for their escape. Canadian and American commandos of *The Devil's Brigade*, also from 1968, climbed a mountain in Italy to attack a Nazi fort. Hollywood's climbing commandos were usually charismatic troublemakers only entrusted with important missions because of a combination of rare skills and suicidal tendencies. I would later learn that climbing in the Allied nations in the 1940s lagged far behind that of Germany, Italy and Austria. If climbing had played as much of a role in the Second World War as it did in movies, the Axis powers would have had a big advantage.

The Victor comics had a strip about my favourite fictional commando climber. Joe Bones, "The Human Fly," was a British crag climber who scaled Nazi alpine hideouts, where his startled enemies would die in a spray of fire from his Sten gun. Joe Bones's name alluded to that of top British cragsman Joe Brown, who was born in Manchester in 1930 and was therefore too young to have fought. Being fictionalized and written into a war story was a very British compliment.

I'd never really felt like I came from Toronto, which was miles away by subway from Etobicoke and, like England, full of different people and more settled, older things than those I grew up with. I didn't dislike the city, but I came from an unsettled suburb still building and destroying itself.

I turned ten the year we sold McGillivray's Hill. I had learned to cross the four-lane black-top of Islington Avenue alone. There, trespassing across a golf course gave me access to creek beds, ravines, parks and golf courses connecting the sub-rural landscape to the north with Lake Ontario. Nature, which had overcome the farmers' attempts to tame it on McGilllivray's Hill, was here reduced to an anemic chain of pockets of woods and marshes on ground too damp or rugged for concrete foundations. In these places, I felt at home.

On stepping stones in a creek, I heard electric church bells tolling from the speakers of an ersatz gothic church on a strip of artificial old-fashioned shops. Citizens of a world that hadn't existed a decade ago shopped there for home-style frozen food and paint that made new furniture look antique. Teachers and television explained this world, but I paid less attention to both than I did to my creeks, woodlots and imagination.

When I was 12, my father's work took us to Switzerland one summer. We rode a funicular railway to a mountain tea room. There were mountaineers with ropes bandoliered across their anoraks and faces reddened by the wind and sun. Their ice axes were strapped to their rucksacks like rifles. Through the window we could see blue glaciers winding down from plains of ice where rock walls shot skyward. Climbers covered their eyes with goggles as thick as welders' and picked their way through boulders towards the glacier. They looked like comic-book heroes, yet they were so real in their connection to the bright, raw world they moved in that I could not imagine them anywhere else.

CHAPTER 2

Suburban Rockcraft

When we came home from England, I returned to the local public school. I liked reading and drawing and was known as an unremarkable daydreamer. Although I wore glasses and was short for my age, I was no clichéd sickly kid. Running everywhere outside made me fit, and I was strong from climbing trees and could throw a football. School sports were rough games meant to teach team spirit and competition rather than the pleasure and benefits of exercise. Despite my fitness, I was shy and independent and participated in them half-heartedly.

My Grade 7 physical education teacher wore a track suit and a whistle, even when he taught math. One afternoon, instead of the usual black-and-white film about the perils of drugs and sex, he showed a documentary about a two-day ascent of the South Face of Washington Column, a high rock wall in Yosemite Valley in California. The climbers had long hair and said "man" a lot, like schoolyard drug dealers in B movies, yet there was nothing laid-back about their high-tech equipment and daredevil manoeuvres. When the lights came back on, the teacher asked if anyone besides him was inspired to try climbing. Perhaps my lacklustre sports record made him sigh when no one raised their hand except me. Climbing, however, didn't resemble any of the sports I knew.

He had a point, though. I was still just a part of the scenery of brick box houses and shopping malls. If I was a bomb set to go off at a later date, no one guessed it. The sense that I could one day be like those climbers was pure hubris.

Most of the time, I kept my dreams and impulses to myself. I had secret crushes on girls I hardly knew. Judy Paddon had long brown hair. Her big yellow dog walked to school on its own every day and sat outside her classroom window until the bell rang and she walked home with him. She was a grade ahead of me, and when she went to high school, the dog still came to the window for her.

While my parents and sisters travelled in Europe, Reg and I went to summer camps on the Canadian Shield, near Parry Sound. We lived in huts, learned to paddle canoes and ate at long trestle tables. The highlight was always backcountry canoe camping. After a day paddling on blue lakes and portaging through the woods, we cooked macaroni and cheese in aluminum pots on crackling fires and slept in mouldy canvas tents.

I first climbed rock at summer camp. Climbing was a trendy addition to outdoor programs meant to encourage teamwork and self-discovery. My first instructor had a salad-bowl-shaped helmet perched on the back of his head, a high voice, a bushy red moustache, some climbing gear that looked pretty cool and a coiled hawser. The rope was the only thing I recognized from Joe Bones's kit.

After the movie about Washington Column, I was a little disappointed that the cliff was only a few feet higher than the trees. Top-ropes – ropes passed through an anchor at the top of the cliff and taken in by a belayer at the bottom to secure a falling climber – were already in place. The instructor showed us how to tie the rope around our waist with a bowline. We later learned to tie a length of nylon webbing into a harness to distribute the load of a fall to our legs, but this seemed unnecessarily complicated. I struggled up the slabs and cracks with no technique, scratching my knees and hands as the white plastic soles of my North Star sneakers skidded on lichen. I got to the top after many falls that left me hanging, but only for moments, since the rope burning into my sides and crushing my guts was incentive to carry on. It must have been an easy climb, but the elation I felt when I finally belly-flopped over the top was more intense than anything I could remember.

We also learned how to rappel down the face by wrapping the rope around our bodies or passing it through a carabiner attached to a harness of cord. My painful rope burns made me admire the high-speed rappellers I had seen in war movies.

Local girls helping in the kitchen undermined the chastening effects of the Nordic landscape. If you were lucky, when they put food on the table, a strand of hair fell on your neck, smelling of talcum and tobacco. One of the girls stood behind the kitchen one night when I walked by. I followed her through the mist to a sandy bank surrounded by rushes.

"You want a rollie or a boughten one?" she asked.

I pointed at the red-and-white packet, although I had only tried a cigarette once before and hated it. Smoke wreathed from her nostrils. Our eyes met for a second and she unbuttoned her shirt. I felt her pulse in my palm. Cigarette still smouldering in her fingers, she put her arm around my neck and kissed me. It seemed like just seconds later that she was doing up her buttons and taking a long drag before tossing the stub of her cigarette in the stream, where it hissed and went out. Years later, she wrote me a letter saying she saw me in the newspaper trying to climb the CN Tower but I probably didn't remember her. I didn't write her back.

A long bus ride took me back to the city, where a thermal inversion made overheated power lines buzz and melted the tarmac streets. Memories of my brief moments climbing were an escape from the growing fear of high school. One afternoon I rode my bike to the public library to see if I could at least find a book about climbing. There, next to the books on tennis and improving your golf swing, was a whole shelf of climbing and mountaineering books. I borrowed as many as I could carry.

The first one I read was *The English Outcrops* by Walter Unsworth. Unsworth's lofty sportsmanship soared above his subjects, which were cliffs mainly no higher than those I had climbed. I was surprised that he didn't consider top-roping, the only climbing I knew, to be climbing at all. As a former reader of *The Victor*, I wasn't surprised that British climbers associated cheating – using pitons and other mechanical techniques – with German and Italian climbers. Scottish mountaineer and war hero W.H. Murray even suggested that pitons could only be used on the rock of a hostile state.

The Seventh Grade, by Italian Reinhold Messner, who avoided pitons and bolts and made fast ascents of giant walls in the Alps, made Unsworth's book seem dated. With his long hair and fashionable clothes, Messner looked like a celebrity. French guide Gaston Rébuffat was well represented in *On Snow and Rock, Men and the Matterhorn* and *Between Heaven and Earth*. Rébuffat's words were philosophical, but the photographs were athletic. They showed him in a red Gallic cap and baggy Tintin knickers, climbing rock faces in the Alps, usually with little safety gear.

The climbers in Galen Rowell's *The Vertical World of Yosemite* had dirty long hair and tackled cliffs as big as those of the Alps, although the walls were surrounded by forests rather than glaciers. It was rock climbing on the grandest scale. The star of the book was a gaunt man with Clark Kent glasses, a beatnik goatee and the unlikely name of Royal Robbins.

Robbins's how-to book, *Advanced Rockcraft*, had cartoons in the style of *Mad* magazine, illustrating how to use ropes and climbing equipment, and the rules climbers called ethics. It was mainly about free climbing – using a minimum of simple equipment only to protect a climber in case of a fall, not as supports or handholds. Robbins saw climbers not only as sportsmen but also as artists. "A first ascent," said Robbins, "is a creation in the same sense as is a painting or a song."

I hadn't read many pages before I decided to try climbing on my own. The library didn't have *Basic Rockcraft*, also by Robbins, so I decided to reverse-engineer climbing practices from advanced ones. Likewise, although there was no book entitled *Easy Rock*, which would have been suitable for a beginner like me, they did have a new copy of *Hard Rock*. The editor, Ken Wilson, whose *Mountain* magazine I would soon discover, had asked top climbers to write about their favourite difficult British rock climbs. Some of the cliffs in the photos reminded me of the ones I had seen on McGillivray's Hill, and I wondered if people had climbed there. I would later find out that several of the climbers from *Hard Rock* had come to Canada for work and climbing, and a few even climbed on the Niagara Escarpment.

The naive belief that I could learn to climb on my own proved a powerful antidote to adolescent suburban boredom. Climbers filled in a gap left by discarded childhood heroes. They could be as idealistic as British commandos in war movies and as cynical and nihilistic as their comic-book enemies.

Among the library's collection were epics about Germans climbing the north face of the Eiger. I had just graduated from war comics to Sven Hassel's novels. Hassel's *Blitzfreeze* and *The Bloody Road to Death* were million-copy bestsellers about an SS penal regiment in Russia. The violence, starvation and frostbite explained why Schultz on TV's *Hogan's Heroes* preferred being a stooge for the American POWs to being sent to the Eastern Front. Hitler's request that Germans conquer the 4,000-foot-high face of the Eiger was fulfilled by real climbers tough enough to be characters in Hassel's books. Some German alpinists fell and some froze on that wall, but the conquerors became mountaineering stars. Austrian SS man Heinrich Harrer was a member of the four-man team to ascend the face, and his book, *The White Spider*, made him a celebrity. Anderl Heckmair, who led the ascent, was in Leni Riefenstahl's propaganda film *Triumph of the Will* and wrote books on the Eiger. Even the British liked a little nihilism with their climbing. A postwar rock-climbing club founded by Joe Brown was named the Valkyries, after the Nordic goddesses who rewarded brave warriors with eternal life.

The alpine epics were outdone in thickness, number of titles and body count by books about Himalayan mountaineering. *Hard Rock*'s earnest climbers' praise for outcrops and condemnation of unsporting practices like using carabiners as handholds seemed Lilliputian next to the heroics in Chris Bonington's *Annapurna South Face*. In 1970 Bonington led the team of crack mountaineers who forged a route up that steep Himalayan face. Few climbers had visited the Himalayas, and no Briton climbed Everest by any route until Bonington's 1975 Everest Southwest Face expedition. Bonington became known for employing dozens of climbers and approaching mountains with a baggage train of porters. Every expedition was followed by a thick book. In Bonington's time, expeditions to major Himalayan peaks were so expensive that it took entire countries to launch them, and a nation's first Everest climbers became national heroes. It was a role that some, but not all, climbers found awkward.

Bonington's men endured sub-zero temperatures, lack of oxygen, breaking ropes and barrages of falling rock and ice. Himalayan mountaineering was as dangerous as the Second World War, but the climbers were cooler than GIs. They had the same hobbies as James Bond – women, drinking, skiing and climbing – pastimes that didn't include a licence to kill but could kill you. In winters they taught skiing in the Alps at places with names like Club Vagabond, and in the summers they climbed in South America and Asia. Despite their silk scarves, deep tans and long hippie hair, they embodied British masculine fortitude.

The two climbers who finished the Annapurna route were Don Whillans, a husky tough from Salford, near Manchester, and the handsome, blue-eyed Scotsman Dougal Haston. Bonington's book about the climb was dedicated "To Ian Clough, who gave so much." Clough was a talented but modest man killed by a falling ice wall on the descent. Haston, a ruthless risk taker, was buried in an avalanche while skiing in Switzerland in 1977. Whatever they had been like in life, dying in the mountains made both these climbers seem like martyrs. In the hot late-August days of 1976, death by climbing was too remote to scare me. Books gave me a pantheon of climbers who, unlike Joe Bones, were real men. They clearly would have preferred death on an alpine wall to floating in a backyard swimming pool drinking beer and waiting for a heart attack.

I had values, inspiration and instructions, but the how-to books said that you needed a climbing partner. Bonington trolled the crags and alpine bars of Europe for devil-may-care climbing geniuses. I knew no climbers, but kids I knew who did dangerous things on bikes, blew things up, climbed hydro towers and snuck into army-supply depots seemed like reasonable substitutes. Chief among these was my brother, Reg. Although our paths would converge later, I didn't ask him to climb because he would have told me that I had no idea what

I was talking about. Also, he had better things to do, having just discovered partying. There was someone who was perfect, however, and I was sure he had nothing better to do than I did.

William Jack and I had been friends since nursery school. We had learned to read and write together, had stabbed, shot and blown each other to bits in play battles, compared Christmas gifts on Boxing Day, survived the same gym classes and been sent to the office together for truancy and minor acts of vandalism. We would both attend Etobicoke Collegiate that September, and neither of us looked forward to it.

William and his brother, Ian, who was a year younger than him, seemed to live joyously rule-free, if occasionally painful, lives. Their mother was red-faced and squat as a beer bottle and spent most of her time watching television in their dusty living room. Stacks of unwashed dishes filled the kitchen, and piles of laundry, old newspapers and boxes of empty bottles lined the hallways. Dinner was often pizza or Chinese food, but when she did buy groceries, the frozen TV dinners in tinfoil trays, bottled pop and aerosol cans of artificial whipped cream created a holiday atmosphere. The brothers always fought over the last can of dessert foam, and the victor sprayed it into his mouth.

There were vicious fights. At one sleepover, the basement television was on late into the night, and we nodded in and out of sleep. When Ian started snoring, William crept over, cinched his sleeping bag tight, poured cola through the hole, dragged him up the stairs and rolled him back down. As Ian screamed and struggled to escape the sleeping bag, William beat him with a golf driver. Ian burst free in his underwear, his hair spiky with cola, his pasty torso mottled with bruises. Snatching the club, he chased William into the street.

The suburban id driving William's family life fed a hunger for spontaneity, and perhaps even chaos, that my home life denied. My father researched the hazards of alcoholism, and my mother was a teetotaller. Even their wedding had been dry. William's mother, however, usually had a drink in hand. His father was a hot-headed insurance salesman who seemed to be trying to cash in policies on his sons. While painting a second-storey window, William spilled paint on his father, who pushed the ladder over. William landed unhurt in a hedge. There were no apologies afterwards and no apparent resentment. I feared my parents' disappointment more than William and Ian feared sudden punishments that might maim or kill them.

William and I had climbed fences to see the stuff on the other side, scaled hydro towers because we were told not to and built homemade fireworks just to see explosions. He didn't fear electrocution, guard dogs, third-degree burns, arrest or reform school, so he wouldn't be too afraid to climb. Would he be safe? I was too ignorant of safety techniques to care. He loved the idea and agreed to go as soon as

I could figure out where we would climb and how we could get some gear.

Camping stores catered mainly to fishermen and hunters, and even in Canada's largest city it wasn't easy to find a decent pair of hiking boots, let alone climbing gear. If I had known where to buy the equipment, I still couldn't have afforded it. I assumed I could improvise and went to Canadian Tire, where most of the outdoor gear in Canada was purchased and where my father had bought his guns.

There, I found four chain links to use as carabiners and ten feet of quarter-inch yellow polypropylene cord for slings. The cord was almost too stiff to knot. A construction site provided some lengths of drilled angle iron that looked like pitons. Canadian Tire didn't have the half-inch nylon hawser I had used at camp, but I knew a railroad supply yard behind a mall that had some green plastic rope that looked about the same diameter. I had just finished stuffing 80 feet of it into my rucksack when I was nabbed by two plainclothes security men. They asked if I had broken into a railway car and checked my pack for stolen TVs. Since I promised not to come back and steal anything else, they let me keep the rope. None of this kit was built for climbing, but it made me feel safer than having nothing.

All I needed now was a place to climb. If you live in Vancouver, Calgary or Munich, you can see where the mountains are. I had to be more resourceful. I found a book about how to stay fit for climbing in London, England (it was part of a series that included a book called *Odd Aspects of England*). It suggested scrambling on everything from the smallest clay creek banks to railway bridges. With enough imagination, the author suggested glowingly, the city provided many "fine opportunities to break one's neck."

I set out to find a cliff high enough to kill a suicide jumper, out of easy reach of adults who might try to stop me and close enough to get to on my bike. The only candidate was the shale outcrop beside the Humber River. I had seen it from a railway bridge we crossed to steal soup-pot-shaped steel helmets from an abandoned army depot.

The underbrush on the bank opposite the cliffs was scored with dirt-bike trails. A riverside footpath was visited only by occasional birdwatchers. It was two miles away from the nearest parking lot – farther than most adults I knew would walk. Neither the bikers nor the birdwatchers were likely to notice us.

William wore workboots without laces. Our rope and his hockey helmet were in his gym bag, and everything else was in my army-surplus haversack. I considered protecting my head with an army helmet, but it was so heavy it hurt my neck. I realized why Joe Bones climbed bare-headed. We thrashed through raspberry cane behind a boarded-up gas station and scrambled down to stone tile between the wall and the river. The cliff's high point was an intimidating overhang of turf and dangling roots. A few yards upriver, near an old shopping cart, the main cliff rose in perfect geology-class strata. Layers of grey shale, clay and soft white limestone led to a final band of brown dirt from which sprung golf courses, malls, acres of tarmac, hair salons and the rest of civilization as I knew it.

With my fake climbing hardware dangling from a hank of yellow cord, I hitched the rope around my waist with a bowline. William put on his helmet and belayed me by running the rope around his butt. An old man watched from the far bank.

I started up the slope, the thin, sharp layers of shale biting into the soles of my sneakers. Twenty feet up, at a vertical step of soft stone, I bashed a piton into a crack with a ball-peen hammer. It only bent a little. Attaching it to the rope with a chain link, I felt cunning. Royal Robbins said in his book that "like a single word in a poem, a single piton can affect the entire composition," and I agreed.

A dozen yards higher, I had climbed so far above my piton that even if it held, and it probably wouldn't have, I would hit the ground before William's belay stopped me. My hands and feet slid on the thin intrusions of dirt between the shale layers. I looked down to see William holding the rope with one hand and skipping rocks at the old man, who yelled that I should come down before I caused an avalanche. Eddies of dust and stones slithered down and zinged in the shopping cart. A trucker somewhere fired his airbrakes.

I realized that despite my criteria for choosing the cliff, I would probably not be killed if I fell, just horribly injured. I was Icarus in an update of the classical picture; just a dot in the Etobicoke sky, the foreground filled with strip malls and golf courses, high-school football games and car dealerships instead of shepherds and temples. We had all heard about teenage hydro-tower climbers fried by high-tension wires or carloads of drunken rowdies pulped by trains. The myth of the kid on drugs who threw himself out of a window because he wanted to fly was so pervasively suggestive that I had a friend who did it after he got drunk. He was lucky; it was a ground-floor window. At least he had drunkenness as an excuse. I blocked out the image of myself as a bloody teenage wipeout. My feet slid and my ankles shook only when I imagined falling, so I padded upwards. I decided not to use another piton, since what had appeared to be a stone block was just a lighter bit of dirt. Soon I was hand-over-handing up a root to the weedy summit.

I tied myself to a thin tree to belay William. Hammerless, he twisted out the piton with his hand, cracking off rock that bounced off his helmet into the river. The old man threatened to call the police, but he stayed and watched.

Memories of the adventure became a sanctuary from boredom for days afterwards. Yet I had no sense of having made a new climbing route. I didn't know that I was entitled to name it, and I certainly could not have graded it. Royal

Robbins said you composed a climb using the cracks and holds on the face to challenge your body, mind and equipment in a way that other climbers found beautiful. My climb wasn't beautiful, but we repeated it many times. We visited the riverbank in fall and winter, climbing, rappelling, shinning up ropes with prusik knots we had seen in crevasse rescue books, and cutting steps in an ice gully with an old ice axe we bought from a ski shop that had been using it as decor. When Reg finally came to try rappelling, a cop ticketing dirt bikers spotted us but was impressed by our railway rope and chain links and left us alone. Reg was less convinced and wouldn't try climbing again for a couple of years.

Thirty years later, I returned to the riverbank. The sliver of woodlot at the top was gone. Asphalt parking lots of 1980s low-rise strip malls crumbled over the cliff edge. Police tape rattled in the trees. The shopping cart was gone, replaced by a car axle and wheel. Shards of windshield glass glinted on the stone tiles. By then I had travelled to many of the world's great climbing cliffs, but although the face had eroded, this one still looked loose and dangerous.

The scarcity of natural suitable outcrops encouraged us to explore artificial topography. Building climbing had a long history. Climbers called it buildering, because, like bouldering, it was mainly done as practice for real rocks and mountains. Edwardian student climbers climbed their colleges for adventure and practice using rock-climbing techniques. Long before Edwardian mountaineering, scaling buildings was a specialized trade in burglary, and although we weren't burglars, we were chronic minor trespassers.

The possibilities for man-made climbing were limited only by imagination and by fear of arrest, drowning, darkness and confined spaces. A network of concrete tunnels, barricades, drainages and bridges kept the roads and basements of the city dry. With flashlights in our hands or teeth, we explored man-sized tubes that ended in walls set with rungs. These led to even smaller tunnels that continued for miles to grates we could open. Underpasses and bridges had cracks we could climb by jamming in our hands and feet. If they were too thin for our hands, we dreamed about scaling them by standing in slings attached to pitons, like big-wall aid climbers in Yosemite or the Alps.

After climbing the Humber cliff we turned our attention to an overpass near Etobicoke Collegiate with a vertical crack in a concrete wall starting ten feet up. It went another ten feet before shooting twenty feet horizontally out the underside of the road to the sunlight. There we could use a projecting rebar as a hook to lower back to the streambed.

To reach the crack, we needed what climbers call a bolt – a metal peg in a drilled hole, used as an anchor for a rope ladder or for protection. Theoretically, with enough bolts and time, anything could be climbed. In practice, however, the number of bolts climbers used was limited because drilling a single hole with a hammer and bit took almost an hour. Bolts appeared in photos of Yosemite or the Alps, but they were barred from British crags, where they were derided as unsporting. Reinhold Messner, who made the first oxygen-free and solo ascents of Everest, scorned them as "murdering the impossible," because they offered a means to overcome holdless rock. Even the bolt we needed for the bridge seemed a little contraband.

While I was searching the bins in the local hardware store for a suitable bolt, I saw my mother buying stencils for her latest redecorating campaign. I looked away as I snuck out empty-handed. Rolling papers and porn magazines were on the secret shopping lists of most teenage boys, but an expansion bolt seemed even more underground, if only because it was to fulfill a less familiar need. I went to a hardware store where I was certain I would meet no one I knew.

The bells on the door were still tinkling as I rushed to the drawers full of nuts, bolts and drill bits. I put a couple of two-inch-long lead shields into a little paper bag along with a six-inch drill bit and some shiny bolts. I avoided clerks, who might ask why I wanted the stuff. All I had to do was show the cashier what was in my little bag, pay and leave.

Behind the cash register stood Tina, who sat next to me in English class. She smiled and after she saw my bolts said she'd never seen me there before and wouldn't have guessed I was the type who did masonry repairs. I laid down three green dollar bills and left. I was embarrassed, but at least I had my first bolt kit.

I spent my lunch hours during the next week below the bridge, standing on shattered concrete and banging the bit with a rock. I couldn't afford the bit's handle, and bringing a hammer to school might get me arrested. After three days, I had made a hole an inch deep. Even with a drill, the impossible didn't die easily.

On Saturday William and I returned with our aid climbing gear: ten homemade angle irons for pitons, hardware-store chain links, thin plastic cord tied into three-step rope ladders and the plastic railway rope. The line drawings I had seen of aid climbing, or what the English disparagingly called mechanical climbing, looked like the paper leaflet instructions for plastic model airplanes. I saw it as just a matter of following some procedures in the right order.

William held the rope patiently while I hammered the shield into the hole. It only went halfway. I screwed in the bolt, attached a sling of thin, yellow, plastic rope and stood in it. The bolt held, but my feet scrabbled on the dusty vertical concrete as I spun down and sideways until my head was at the five o'clock position. I righted myself and pushed the tip of a piton into the fracture.

Hammering the piton was so tiring that when it was only partway in I attached my other rope ladder to it with a chain link. My left foot was numb and I wanted to step up and take weight off it. Dirt dribbled from the crack below the piton, but the piton held my weight. I wondered why all the books said free climbing – just using hands and feet on the natural holds on a cliff face – was harder than aid climbing. After two more pitons I reached the roof. We had four left, so I reckoned I could get all the way out to the rebar if I placed one every five feet. I was getting ready to hammer a piton into the roof when William said he wanted to lead.

He'd never led before, and I tried to talk him into waiting and trying something else, but between aiding highway underpasses and free climbing on shale cliffs, I couldn't think of anything we would climb that would be easier. I came down.

It took him an hour to reach the roof and hammer in another piton. Joined to the piton by a chain link, he hung horizontally, pushing his feet against the wall, reaching out with another piton, seeming weightless as an astronaut. But then a truck a couple of feet above rocked the bridge, and the pitons ripped out. With an echoing crash, William landed on his back, frozen in his climbing position, staring silently upwards.

Tina's brother, Bruno, ran around the corner from the next bay of the underpass. He had a mickey of liquor-board rum. Nudging William with his boot, he said he looked totally fucked, then left. After a couple of minutes, William coughed, blinked and got up. A hole in the back of his flannel jacket made a red flap. We left the chain link and piton, which might still be there, pulled down the rope and left, never to return. I wouldn't aid climb again for years.

The next time I saw Tina, she smirked while I pretended to write in my notebook.

From then on, we mostly climbed city works buildings faced with slabs of red-and-grey Canadian Shield granite. They had actual handholds and were usually hidden in parks, where no one would see us. Traversing on their real rock facades actually strengthened our fingers and improved our footwork.

My search for a cliff where I wouldn't skid to my death in a dust devil of shale, or impale myself on rebar, led to one of the important discoveries of my life: the library copy of Jim Mark's *Rock Climbing in Southern Ontario*. On the red dust jacket, a disembodied sheep's head floated above a shield with a mantle of climbing rope. This was the coat of arms of the Alpine Club of Canada, one of the oldest organizations of its kind in the world. The club's Toronto Section was the book's publisher.

The club was founded in Winnipeg in 1906. The completion of the Trans-Canada Railroad and a chain of resort hotels had just given Eastern Canadians, Americans and Europeans access to the Rocky Mountains. The Alpine Club in London had been founded by Victorian British urbanites who climbed in the European Alps, and the Alpine Club of Canada allowed Canadian city dwellers with a penchant for mountains to explore the vast Rockies. The club's Toronto Section was founded only a few years after the national club. Some of its members were European immigrants used to practicing on small crags. The granite of the Canadian Shield and the Niagara Escarpment offered them fine practice for mountain climbing.

By the time Mark wrote his book, there were a couple of hundred climbs on a dozen Ontario cliffs. Most of these, including Kelso, Rattlesnake Point and Mount Nemo, were on the Niagara Escarpment, near Milton, an hour's drive from Toronto. The book's longest chapter covered the three-hundred-foot face of Mazinaw Rock, which was also called Bon Echo. The section owned a hut there, but since it was three hours northeast of the city by car and I was too young to drive, it was definitely too far away for me. Climbs were graded according to their level of difficulty, from 5.0 to 5.11, the hardest climb in the guidebook.

Many different systems have been invented to grade rock climbs. They let climbers know what to expect on a given climb and how their skills compare to those of other climbers. The system used in most places in North America was, and still is, the Yosemite Decimal System. It starts at 5.0 (the 5 never changes; it's a remnant of a part of the system that also rated scrambling on non-technical ground) and proceeds to 5.9. At this point, for a reason no one knows, instead of going to 6.0, it goes to 5.10. Routes 5.10 and up are often assigned a letter grade between *a* and *d* (i.e., 5.10c) to reflect shades of difficulty within the grade itself. Grades are added as harder and harder climbs are done. At time of writing, the hardest climb in the world is 5.15, but in 1975, it was 5.12.

Even though I had no idea what grade I climbed, some of the route names intimidated me. What hid behind the bland descriptiveness of the Chimney or Yellow Groove? Simply adding someone's name to the described feature made it seem much more impressive. Alan's Layback implied that Alan had made a heroic effort. Others, like Dilly Dally and Birthday Ridge, seemed playful and harmless, but were they? Monikers like Freefall, the Spider and Glue Party, on the other hand, were warnings or dares. I wondered what adventures these routes might offer as I shovelled snow and delivered papers to get enough money to buy genuine climbing equipment so I could try them.

In spring I rappelled down the shale cliffs on the green plastic rope one last time. I threw the chain-links in the river and dumped the rest in the shopping cart and set fire to it. As a climber on real cliffs, I would still be something of a pretender, but at least my gear would be real.

In a dim corner of Margesson's sports store on Adelaide Street in Toronto, carabiners, black steel pitons and aluminum protection wedges known as nuts hung on wall hooks. A reel of nylon hawser and tightly coiled European kernmantle ropes lay on the floor. As I toyed with the equipment, I was joined by a boy with the faint beginnings of a black moustache. His hair came to his shoulders, and his nylon backpack was covered with patches from mountain clubs and rock bands.

He said his name was Steve Labelle and he asked if I climbed in the area. He hadn't seen me at Rattlesnake Point, where the action was. He dropped the names of a few of his friends – George Manson, Dave Lanman, Mike Tschipper – as if I should know them. They were going to the Valley in the summer. I had read about Yosemite but didn't know that climbers called it the Valley, so I nodded as if I knew what he was talking about. I had difficulty just getting to local cliffs and hoped he wouldn't ask me what grade I climbed. I hadn't prepared to meet someone who was going to Yosemite.

I followed his lead and bought a copy of the English magazine *Mountain*. The rope, carabiners, nuts and smooth-soled French climbing shoes I acquired that summer made it possible to climb, but *Mountain* told me how and why I should bother. It covered everything from rock climbing in California to Himalayan mountaineering and was filled with images of extreme climbing and gossip about climbs and climbers. Its writers devoted as much ink to topics like whether pitons or chalk should be used on small cliffs as they did to the controversy over hanging miles of fixed ropes on giant mountains.

Mountain showed that the books I had read by Rébuffat,

Bonington and Robbins were out of date. Bonington was seen as unfashionably nationalistic, his expeditions were criticized for being too hierarchical and his need for publicity was lampooned. In *Mountain* climbers protected themselves with nuts placed by hand, rather than the pitons and wooden wedges Rébuffat had hammered into the Alps. Unlike Robbins, the climbers had long hair and looked like hippies, except that their muscles bulged beneath their T-shirts. I stopped cutting my hair and started doing pull-ups and running.

My transition from an unkempt, skinny daydreamer to an unkempt, slightly more muscular, high-school daydreamer was gradual. To those unfamiliar with *Mountain* – which was everyone – my hair made me look like the stoners in the smoking area outside the school cafeteria. My parents started wondering whether the camp with rock climbing had been a good idea.

In the spring of 1977, I started climbing on the Niagara Escarpment, near Milton. A Puritan farmer had named the town after John Milton, the author of *Paradise Lost*. The only famous thing that had happened there was the invention of the Robertson screw. The rocks of the neighbouring Niagara Escarpment, the same feature that formed McGillivray's Hill, 80 miles to the north, were so neglected that climbers from the cities to the west and south had to name most of them themselves.

North of the highway was Cow Crag, named after a cattle

pasture that became a golf course. To the south was Kelso, with its abandoned yellow quarry and grey prow of natural stone. From there, the green mesa curved round to where Rattlesnake Point basked in the sun. Although there had once been timber rattlesnakes there, the cliff actually took its name from the serpentine curve of the mesa. Its neighbour, Buffalo Crag, overlooked a pen of buffalo, also now gone. Across Limestone Creek, only a sliver of overhanging Punk Rock was visible above the trees. Below Rattlesnake, Nassagaweya Canyon's bower of orchards and fields sloped three miles southwards to the long wall of Mount Nemo, which appeared from miles around to terminate in a huge overhang.

Even though Steve said Rattlesnake was where all the action was, I chose Kelso for the same reason that made it one of the first cliffs climbed near Milton: I had seen it from Highway 401, the road stretching from Detroit to Montreal that served as Toronto's major east-west artery. This was important, because William and I were only 14 and our parents had to drop us off in the morning and pick us up at the end of the day. It was a two-hour round-trip. My father usually did it first thing on Sunday morning, and William's father came to get us in the afternoon.

My father listened to the opera on the radio as he drove. Years later, he told me he had expected William and I would be killed on our climbs. I was surprised, because he had once rappelled down a small cliff and hadn't seemed frightened, although he never tried it again. For years afterwards my mother complained about how dirty he'd made his jacket.

My parent's misgivings about climbing didn't decrease my enthusiasm. Fascination with the cliffs and joy at being able to climb them, however badly, confirmed my feeling that I had discovered the key to my satisfaction and happiness.

With packs full of climbing gear and sandwiches wrapped in waxed paper, we walked up through the birches to the old quarry floor. A shattered ochre wall rose above rusted mining equipment and tailings. Although we sometimes climbed there, we preferred the solid, naturally exposed rock face a few minutes farther on.

Kelso was in Mark's guidebook. The routes had names and grades, and climbers had painted little numbers on the cliff to help find them. Pitons sticking out from cracks or from overhangs I couldn't imagine climbing were reminders of Kelso's modest place in the history of climbing. The steepest and best climbs at Kelso came in the late 1950s, when many Europeans from alpine countries settled in Canada. They knew tricks I had seen Rébuffat do in books, like switching between standing in rope ladders and climbing on the rock's natural holds, or placing pitons one-handed. Some were also champion fencers. Their central-European names – Boris, Helmut, Hans – were in the first-ascent records of many Canadian climbing guidebooks.

We were less dashing. Huddling in the shade below the overhangs in our flannel jackets and green work pants from the Zellers discount store, we looked more like window cleaners than climbers. William's eyes were hidden by the cherry-red fibreglass climbing helmet that had replaced his hockey helmet. He pulled the rope through a belay hitch in a carabiner that kinked it like a stretched-out slinky because we never tied it right. I tried to place my protection the way that I had seen it done in books and to guess how the climbers in *Mountain* moved. We tried any techniques we could find, and luckily they often worked.

The crag was no longer popular with climbers, partly because it faced north and was cold for much of the year, unlike nearby, south-facing Rattlesnake Point. Only once did we meet other climbers. Two men with beards, ropes and corduroy knickers apprehensively watched through their wire-rimmed glasses as William led a climb.

After a half-hour struggle, William reached an overhang and decided to lower back down. He placed a nut in a crack and clipped it to the rope. It was all that protected him from falling to the ground, but it tore out, sending him flying. It was the second time I saw a bush save him from the impact of a fall, but the accident with the ladder had been more dangerous; this time he had only been ten feet up. The onlookers gasped, not at our bravery but at our incompetence.

"When you're practicing like this, you should think about whether you could do that kind of thing on a real mountain," one said.

It was good advice, but I wasn't practicing for something else. I knew mountains only from books. I satisfied my appetite for climbing with what was available. My lack of knowledge and experience constantly put me in threatening situations that made rocks seem very real. I clipped fixed pitons no matter how old, buckled or rusty they were, assuming that they had been placed by someone who knew more than me. Books showed pictures of nuts fitting in cracks as smoothly as keys in locks. Actually, it was so hard to find cracks that fit the nuts I had that I often skipped placing them, hoping for an old piton higher up.

The best part, however, wasn't using equipment but grabbing the cool grey stone or jamming my arms in a crack that smelled of moss and scuffed my hands. Learning a trick of movement was its own reward. It was exhilarating to pull off a fancy move, like a layback, and then look down the rope to see the vertical cliff face dropping to the shadowy forest.

When we had done all the routes at Kelso, we were still intimidated by the reputation of Rattlesnake Point, so we moved on to Mount Nemo instead. Many mountains are named after famous people. Even Kelso was named after a British lord. Sometime in the early 19th century, farmers began referring to the cliffs north of Burlington as Mount Nemo. Nemo means *nobody* in Latin. As a mountain, it was a bit of a nobody, with forests scarred by the ruins of a quarry and its outbuildings, and pristine outcrops marred by a couple of gullies filled with trash. There were few visitors. The cliff, however, was miles long and higher than other local cliffs. In places it was as loose as rock can get, which explained why alpinists had practiced there in the 1960s, and why the growing field of rock specialists avoided it in the decades before bolt protection was widely accepted. Here, the guidebook was almost useless, and nobody was around to help us find the routes. Taking on unknown climbs meant we backed off a lot, but we also learned a little about route-finding and climbing down.

It wasn't long before climbing was going better than school. In the battleship-grey classrooms of Etobicoke Collegiate, I floundered in science and mathematics and only just passed other subjects. As the months wore on, my lack of success led to an indifference shared by many fellow students. Some of the teachers were just as unhappy. One homeroom teacher burst into tears every morning when the bell rang; another used a driver to lob golf balls at his pupils; another went away with the police.

If you were late, failed a course, were disliked by a teacher or broke school rules, you ended up in the office. There, the vice-principal, with his brown suit and slicked-back hair, told you that if you failed to fit in you were doomed. Some of his problem people could be reclaimed. Scrappers had a role initiating freshmen and playing football. Bad girls might be inspiring cheerleaders. Dope smokers, however, were just arrested and expelled.

The vp didn't see the difference between skipping school to climb and skipping school to drink or drag race and gave me a schedule of detentions. I spent them fantasizing that I was more than a teenage loser avoiding the boredom of school with an obscure thrill. I daydreamed that climbing threatened the vp's thousand-year Reich of televised golf, swimming pools, tranquillizer-numbed housewives and tv dinners. I daydreamed that when the Russians were done painting Africa and Central America red, they would come to Etobicoke and put an end to the counter-revolutionary high-school football team, the recently invented pill-format doughnut called the Timbit and the vp. Then, there would be no problem doing whatever I wanted and climbing all the time.

These fantasies hid a conflict within me. Most people said that high school and the world it prepared kids for was all that existed. I thought I was made for something else, that no one, as yet, understood, but me If I excelled at that special thing, I would escape and become myself, which I did not see as a humble goal. Stoners, school toughs and people in Bruce Springsteen songs were being torn apart by those voices, but not me. I read *Mountain* magazine. I was becoming visible and couldn't help it if people didn't like what they saw.

The numerous and inevitable days without climbing taught me patience. Sometimes I had worries caused only by having to wait to climb. If I wanted to do a climb, I convinced myself that it would be easy, or battered my confidence by imagining difficulties I knew nothing about. Dealing with these feelings fed my new obsession as much as the act of climbing itself.

My parents and sisters spent the summer after my freshman year in Mexico. I got a job as a counsellor at a camp with a climbing program. The instructor knew even less than me, so I did a lot of the belaying, tying kids to ropes and showing them basic movements on the rock. By the end of the summer, I had climbed every inch of the little practice cliff many times and was happy to leave. I wasn't homesick. I was eager for William and me to make our first climbing trip to Bon Echo.

Longing to be one of the ant-like climbers on huge cliffs I had seen in books, I practiced new techniques like stopping to belay halfway up the crag. The rope tangled and my nut anchor fell out on its own. Instead of feeling incompetent, I decided that this had been the best way to learn why books said I should have used two anchors.

Other climbing areas were the subject of epic tales that cautioned rash climbers, but the Milton cliffs were not. Most of the victims of the cliffs were drunks, untrained daredevils or partiers. One morning in Kelso quarry we followed gasoline vapours to a wrecked motorcycle. A local kid had driven it off the quarry top the night before. But nothing would happen to us. We had a rope and knew not to drive off the cliff on a motorcycle. The first local climbing fatality I heard of was a man who had fallen to his death from Rattlesnake Point while setting up a top-rope. When my mother heard about it on the radio, I assured her that I never top-roped, but left out details about my lead climbing.

William's parents drove us to Mazinaw Lake, where his father sat in an aluminum boat, watching his fishing float bob, while his mother worked her way through a case of beer on the beach. A man with a beard and knickers drew alongside the marina dock in the Alpine Club boat. We hopped in with our two small packs and he asked William, "Did I see you take a grounder at Kelso?"

"Never heard of the place," William said.

Stiff from a night on the ground in our thin hardware-store sleeping bags, we sat in the hut, eating from a cereal box. We counted and recounted our carabiners as middle-aged men drank coffee from cone-shaped aluminum cups, pulled on heavy boots and rattled slings of nuts and pitons.

The boat was so full of climbers that the gunwales were only a few inches above the lake as we puttered along below the wall. Someone suspiciously eyed our tiny selection of carabiners and nuts. I was proud of my gear, however, since none of it came from the Canadian Tire store. William was asked about the divot in the side of his helmet.

"A shale brick hit it," William said. "Ever been to the Humber River cliff? It's a riot." The expression on the faces of most of the climbers suggested they had not.

From a distance, Mazinaw Rock appeared to be a clean vertical slice in the earth's crust, but close up it revealed diagonal intrusions of soft grey stone, steep red corners, black ramps and ridges. Orange and green lichen splotched the walls, and I could see a couple of pitons and nylon slings high on the face. One of the climbers pointed to red pictographs scrawled on the rock a millennium before by young braves coming of age. They depicted war canoes and a spirit-man whose head sprouted an antler.

The rock had always cast a spell. It had been painted many times by members of the Group of Seven. In the early 20th century, psychic and revolutionary Flora MacDonald bought the cliff and dedicated it to Walt Whitman with a 20-foot-high inscription carved in the face. When she died, she left it to her son, Merrill Denison. After a couple of Anglo-Canadian doctors and their girlfriends climbed the cliff in 1957, Denison wrote a letter congratulating them. Soon after Denison bequeathed Bon Echo to the Ontario government for parkland, and the Alpine Club purchased property north of the cliff and a boat to get to it.

Everyone wanted us to climb Birthday Ridge, the route the doctors had followed on the first ascent of the cliff. Its grade of 5.1 seemed too easy, and I asked for something harder. We were dropped off on a lake-washed ledge at the foot of a grey ridge. Above was One Pine, which, at 5.3, should have been almost as easy for us as Birthday Ridge.

William belayed as I wandered up a slab, guessing where the holds led. I had few long slings, so the rope zigzagged back and forth across the face until I couldn't pull it up. I stopped just short of the ledge, where I was supposed to belay. After clumsily tying, untying and retying the belay, I brought William up and was ready to lead again. The real belay ledge was spacious and had a piton and a horn of rock to use as anchors, but since it was only a couple of yards above my first belay, I kept climbing.

There were big holds, but the space growing below made the climbing exhilarating. I tiptoed across a ledge to a crack ending at the tree that gave the route its name. Suddenly I couldn't move. I had learned my lesson about rope drag and placed only a few pieces of protection, all in a straight line, so I assumed William wasn't paying attention and yelled for him to feed me more slack. He shouted up that I had climbed to the end of the rope.

My foothold was good, but I couldn't stand on it without holding on. Because we had only climbed on cliffs shorter than our 150-foot line, we didn't know about warning the leader before the rope ran out. I could see a nice ledge perhaps ten yards of easy climbing above me. I cursed William for not telling me I was running out of rope farther down. Then I saw the belay ledge I had missed below.

I put the only nut I had left into the crack. Easing my weight onto it, I remembered that I was supposed to use two anchors, but had no choice but to rely on a single, tiny piece of metal. I wedged my foot into the crack to take some weight off the nut and squeezed the last inch of rope into a belay hitch.

As he climbed, William bounced up and down on the rope. The nut shifted a little. I told him to stop falling, as if he was doing it on purpose. Finally, his helmet came into view below. Every few feet, he had hung on the rope, even where there were ledges to stand on. While I vacillated between the false sensation that the anchor was coming out and just being pissed off with William, the climbers' boat appeared below.

The boatman cupped his hands and hollered; were we all right? I didn't really know the answer, but I gave him the thumbs-up and waved him away as William reached my belay.

"I think we fucked up," he said. "We're in the wrong place and I couldn't get two of the nuts out and I dropped my glasses at the ledge and had to tug on the rope to get them."

I scrambled to the top without placing nuts. The security of sunny ledges, sprawling junipers and terraces of glossy green blueberry bushes made me forget about our errors. Partway back to the hut, the boat's engine cut out and we drifted quietly below climbers on Sweet Dreams. First climbed by the British expat climber John Turner, it was graded 5.8, but some said it was closer to 5.10. It had been one of the hardest climbs on the continent when it was first climbed in 1960.

Turner's other masterpiece at Bon Echo was the Joke, a difficult and dangerous climb that everyone aspired to but few did. I eventually climbed the Joke and some of his other routes at the Shawangunks, north of New York City; the Adirondacks, in upstate New York; the White Mountains of New Hampshire; and the Purcell Mountains of British Columbia. They were all considered pretty tough when he climbed them, and his climbs at Bon Echo were still renowned.

Sweet Dreams traversed a wall leaning over the lake and overcame a black overhang and a sword-cut crack in a vertical wall. The climbers wore jeans and smooth-soled, canvas-topped rock shoes. The leader's ponytail blew in the wind. He looked down and waved, then hauled himself over the overhang. This first real glimpse of hard climbing filled me with an urgent desire to do it myself.

I tried to convince William that we should try Sweet Dreams because we had done a climb of the same grade at Kelso. He said I was crazy, and we silently ate our dinner of Spam on Wonder Bread as the other climbers drank red wine and reflected on the day's adventures.

"So, you were the leader today?" a man with a goatee asked in an accent I couldn't place. "You aren't supposed to belay there, but on the ledge. I can show you in the guidebook. Where did you fellows learn to climb?"

"Kelso, Mount Nemo, you know, around there." I didn't

mention aid climbing on the underpass. William had already told someone about the shale cliffs, so I left that out too.

"Where are you from?"

"Etobicoke."

I looked at the pictures of the snowy Rockies on the walls. I recognized some of the peaks because they were also on $20 bills. Wool knickers and lugged climbing boots made most of the climbers in the hut look like they would fit into that scene better than the granite highlands of the Canadian Shield, where our worlds had come to briefly overlap.

Later that evening I met Norbert, a relaxed graduate student with a beard and a ponytail who had climbed Mount Robson, the highest peak in the Rockies. He wanted to know if I would climb Sweet Dreams with him, and he didn't ask about how I had learned to climb. Crucially, he seemed to know nothing about my fiasco on One Pine.

The next day, William watched us from the boat. After a simple ramp, I led a steep traverse. My rock shoes stuck to the footholds, I didn't run out of equipment before I finished my rope-length, we belayed in the right places, neither of us fell off and we left no equipment behind. It felt triumphant.

That night, back home in my bedroom, I admired the cuts on my hands from Sweet Dreams. As I coiled my rope, Roger Waters's lonely voice whispered on my transistor radio about climbing a hill in his own way. In a month I would be 15, and I had already found what I was going to dedicate my life to.

Even though my second high-school year began in the morning, I couldn't stop smiling.

CHAPTER 3

Middle-Earth

The School of Experiential Education (SEE, as it was usually called) occupied an old schoolhouse in a neighbourhood best known for a gun factory, a sewage-treatment plant and lakefront motels popular with prostitutes. The location enhanced the school's bohemian mystique as a haven for students who were either too rebellious or too brilliant for the drudgery of conventional secondary education. I was there for a more mundane reason: my marks at Etobicoke Collegiate were poor, and I skipped school to climb so often that the school administration threatened suspension. I worried that if that happened, my parents would curtail my climbing.

Rochdale College, Toronto's free university, had closed two years ago, but its hippie atmosphere lived on at SEE. On its walls, students had painted everything from Beatles lyrics to the dance of death from Ingmar Bergman's *The Seventh*

Seal. Students addressed teachers by their first names. The textbooks were written by Kurt Vonnegut, Carlos Castaneda, Joseph Heller and Karl Marx. Some of them would have been confiscated if they had turned up in locker searches at Etobicoke Collegiate. At SEE, however, there was no VP. Students attended classes for a day or so a week and did all their written work on their own.

This light schedule left time for listening to esoteric music, shopping for suede jackets and opera scarves, growing your hair and smoking dope. Driver's licences were tokens of maturity at regular schools, but hardly anyone at SEE had one, so there were no idling Trans Ams with heavy metal blaring from their radios. *Zen and the Art of Motorcycle Maintenance* was taught in English, but only as a metaphor; there were no real motorcycles in the parking lot either.

My long hair was copied from climbers in *Mountain*, but it made some people think I was a stoner, which was a good reputation to have at SEE. Smoking suburban marijuana proved that you were willing to break the law, but did little else. Most of it was grown furtively in backyards was and only slightly more mind-expanding than Canadian foam-filter cigarettes. The cultivation, acquisition and smoking of cannabis were even more popular conversational topics than they were at Etobicoke Collegiate.

There were no school teams or physical education classes. Just being fit enough to do sports was so uncool that I told no one about the running and pull-ups I did for climbing. When a teacher tried to organize some casual cross-country running, a colleague called him a fascist in front of the other students. Climbing itself, however, was weird enough to have cachet. When we learned in class that beatnik poets sometimes climbed mountains, a boy with the unusual name of Brandy Greenwood said he understood. He climbed too.

After class, I told him I was a rock climber and he asked me to share what would be my first joint. Brandy said his father, who lived in Alberta, taught him to climb and suggested I meet up with him and his friends at Rattlesnake Point. I said I had been to Kelso and Bon Echo and tried to make Sweet Dreams sound impressive, but he'd never heard of it. He invited me to a party at his house on the weekend. There would be beer. When he tired of relighting the joint I was constantly letting go out, he showed me a few boulder problems he'd worked out on the brick edges of the school's facade. I couldn't do any of them.

I had seen a photo of his father, Brian Greenwood, climbing a wall in Yosemite. Like Brandy, he had thick lips, long hair and massive hands, which made him look a little Nordic. He had emigrated from Yorkshire to Calgary in the 1950s. The Canadian Rockies guidebooks credited him with the first ascents of dozens of difficult rock climbs and dangerous mountain walls.

A couple of years before I met Brandy, his father retired

from climbing after an ascent of El Capitan, a huge wall in Yosemite. When I climbed in the Rockies, I found out that he had used the names of the monsters and villains from J.R.R. Tolkien's novels for his rock climbs on the steep walls of Mount Yamnuska. In contrast, his children were named after Middle-earth's heroes and heroines. Brandy's sister, Arwen, was a thin beauty with golden hair and fine features. She went to SEE as well.

Any shyness I felt on the night of the party was outweighed by fear that the offer to drink beer with climbers would never be repeated.

Brandy's mother greeted me in a patrician accent and showed me to the dining room, where Brandy gave me my first bottle of beer. I was glad that the music was loud and I could just nod instead of contributing to the conversation. Steve Labelle was there, talking about Dave Lanman, whose ascents of Space Case, a 5.11 at Rattlesnake, and the three-thousand-foot-high Shield route in Yosemite amazed Steve equally. The Shield, Steve explained, had a crux where you had to use 35 RURP pitons, each about the size of a postage stamp. If one RURP pulled, you could tear out the rest and fall a hundred feet. Steve speculated, understandably but incorrectly, that at 16, Dave had been the youngest climber to ascend El Capitan.

With a beer in one hand, Brandy aped Dave Lanman climbing the vaunted overhang of Space Case. I still couldn't picture the climb, but I assumed that if Dave could do it, he was a sort of rock star. Brandy took out his cigarettes and said the hardest part was dangling from a hold the same size as the pack of smokes.

Steve and Dave lived with their families in the same high-rise apartment building, near the highway. After a few hours' climbing at a summer camp, Dave had pestered his father, a former hill runner from England, to find a way for him and his older brother, Steven Lanman, to climb. His dad convinced the Alpine Club to take Steven to their hut at Bon Echo, but Dave was younger than the club's minimum age requirement. Steven participated in a first ascent and came back raving about it. Frustrated, Dave and Steve Labelle resorted to rappelling off a high balcony, but the superintendent caught them. To prevent a repeat of the incident, Dave's father got them a few pieces of gear and a rope and started driving them to Rattlesnake Point. There, Dave discovered a hidden talent and the friendship of experienced mentors like George Manson, about whom Steve also talked a lot.

After the party, a little drunk, I snuck back into my house. Leafing through Jim Mark's guidebook, I noticed how many fewer pages there were about Kelso than about Rattlesnake Point. The notes I had written beside the descriptions seemed childish, the grades of the climbs I had done pitifully low. My efforts had yet to do justice to my dreams. That night, I met kids from neighbourhoods like mine who had become climbers of stature on the same rocks as me. I would not waste the lucky coincidence of that evening; I would do as they had done.

Anticipation made the winter pass slowly. When the spring of 1978 finally came, and William Jack and I walked down the path from the Rattlesnake Point parking lot to the cliff, I felt a mixture of fear and relief. Daydreaming was over, and the test of my will would now begin.

The overhangs of the routes H2S and McMaster Special jutted above the brown ledges separating the east and west cliffs. A few pitons stuck out of smooth rock. A spatula-shaped pinnacle was split by a crack you could see through and climb on both sides. Apparently geologists said it could fall down at any time, but two parties were climbing it anyway.

Farther along, a spring gurgled from a hollow below the tallest part of the cliff. A tree rose by the water, shading an overhanging crack. Piles of climbing gear glinted on a picnic table. The wall was steep and flecked with tiny holds and pockets stained white with gymnast's chalk. I had seen photos of climbers drying sweaty fingers in chalk bags hanging from their waists but had never used chalk myself. It was here that I saw my first real climbing bolt.

A man in a nylon bivouac hammock clipped to a piton a few feet up squirmed free and fell to the ground. A beard ringed his round face, and he had a folded handkerchief tied around his head. His spotless white pants and button-down shirt made William whisper that he looked like Mr. Clean, but he said his name was Bryan. We almost salivated over his hoard of spotless new gear. Even the three nuts I had purchased to replace the ones William had left behind at Bon Echo were already pockmarked. My ten carabiners were so familiar that I could have picked them out of a pile of a hundred by their little scars and the way each gate sprung closed.

Clean climbing – the use of nuts placed and removed by hand – had been brought to North America from Britain. The cliffs went quiet as nuts replaced the steel pitons that had been hammered in and out of the rock, often scarring the cracks on popular climbs. At first, climbers used machine nuts threaded with rope; hence the term *nuts*. Early purpose-built nuts made by British companies like MOAC and Peck were strong but didn't fit cracks well. Yvon Chouinard, who had invented chrome steel pitons that aggravated the scarring problem, designed the first functional protection pieces – tapered Stoppers and eight-sided Hexcentrics. Smaller sizes were threaded with wire swaged into a loop, and larger ones were threaded with loops of rope. Even for climbs ten times as high as Rattlesnake Point, 15 nuts was considered sufficient. Throw in a dozen crudely finished carabiners and a few five-foot-long slings of white tubular webbing, and you had enough equipment for most rock climbs of the time.

The swami belt, a ten-foot length of webbing wrapped around the belly and tied with a water knot, was the usual harness. It was strong, foolproof, let you move freely and looked cool, since it implied that you were tough enough to absorb a fall with the soft part of your abdomen. Sewn harnesses were also gaining acceptance. The Whillans harness, designed by the English climber of the same name, had a strap that looked like it was going to crush your testicles if you fell, but never did. Its orange-and-white webbing, tacked together with thick thread, made it look like it was designed for emergencies. The only headgear serious crag climbers wore was a bandana. Some leading climbers said helmets made climbing more dangerous, as if they magnetically attracted falling rock.

Bryan knew every climb. He pointed to a jagged crack with a small overhang halfway up. It was called Finale, although it was everyone's first climb at the cliff. Remembering what happened when I turned down the classic introduction at Bon Echo, I decided to follow tradition and climb it.

Clanking off across the talus, Bryan said he was going to belay Richard Massiah, who he named as if I should know him, although we hadn't met, on a 5.9 up a thin overhanging crack in white rock. I had never seen someone climb that hard, so I was a little disappointed that a top-rope hung doubled through a carabiner at the top of the cliff.

Richard Massiah was the best climber I had yet seen. He had frizzy long hair and glasses, and although he was the same age as me, he looked like a little kid. Bryan was in the same class as Richard, but he looked too old for high school, and he almost was. He had repeated some grades. They met at high school. Richard had seen the climbing movie *Solo* and wanted to try climbing but was too young for the only available courses; Bryan, who had learned to climb at summer camp, was eager to have a partner and generous with his advice and patience.

Although he and Richard attended upper-middle-class Northern Secondary uptown, Bryan lived in Regent Park, a frankly notorious government-housing development downtown. It was a familiar scenario. My own mother didn't care what courses Reg and I took, but she cajoled us to travel miles to the hilariously named Richview, a school in a wealthier neighbourhood, then attended by future prime minister Stephen Harper. We ignored her and went to lower-middle-class Etobicoke Collegiate, a couple of blocks away.

I soon learned that Richard was a good lead climber, but I couldn't help noticing that most of the people at Rattlesnake were top-roping like he was, albeit on much easier climbs. Many wore baseball caps under their helmets, and some of the belayers refreshed themselves from coolers full of beer and sandwiches. Onlookers heckled or cheered climbers who spent as much time hanging on the rope to rest as they did climbing. They were having fun, but it wasn't for me. I didn't care that in some places top-roping was seen as cheating, I just didn't want climbing to be that safe.

Finale was steeper but easier than I expected. After a brief struggle at an overhang, there were open cracks and ledges and a spacious belay. I envied the skill of the climbers who had left chalk marks on a pencil-thin ledge on the lip of an overhang beside us. I didn't know it, but the chalk was on Space Case.

That afternoon we watched George Manson climb it. Like a sportscaster, Steve Labelle mixed the route's lore into a running commentary on George's ascent. Mike Tschipper and Rob Rohn, two of Steve's friends, had made the first free ascent, climbing with only their hands and feet on the natural holds and cracks and clipping the rope into protection, only to catch a potential fall where others had used pitons as holds. The experience of free climbing a route was so different than using the equipment for aid that routes were sometimes renamed after being free climbed.

Space Case had been known as the Way We Were to the men who had climbed it first, wearing heavy mountain boots and dangling piton hammers. It was impossible to imagine them naming their route Space Case, or even saying the weird names George and his friends gave their climbs: Funky Fingers, When Shrimps Learn to Whistle, Smegma Spasmodic Frog in the Farflung Islets of Langerhans. At Bon Echo the renaming of free routes eventually aroused conflict when older climbers refused to allow a particularly outrageous new name to be recorded in the log and eventually the guidebook.

George's group dressed like the climbers in *Mountain*, with torn jeans, long hair and bandanas. Their most distinctive piece of equipment was the chalk bag hanging from the swami belt, since chalk was associated with a combination of sweat-inducing danger and small holds. Without their permission, familiarity with their lives outside of climbing or even much conversation, I made them mentors, modelling my dress, climbing and speech on them.

Tom Gibson, a friend of George's, was born and raised close to the boulder-strewn mountains near Poway, north of San Diego. Next to his friend Greg Cameron's backyard swing set were two-storey-high granite boulders where they practiced for the mountains of the Sierra and the big walls of Yosemite. As teenagers, the pair joined other local kids to make some early repeat ascents in Yosemite and counted among their occasional climbing partners the Stonemasters, the best rock climbers in the world.

The Stonemasters were technically more skilled than George and his friends, but they also seemed cooler. They were connected to the West Coast's cultural capital in the San Francisco Bay area, just a few hours' drive from Yosemite, the centre of the rock-climbing universe. The Poway Mountain Boys, as Tom, Greg and their friends were known, came from the sprawling suburban San Diego area where the main employer was the navy. The Stonemasters' athletic ascents of the soaring cliffs of Yosemite, Suicide and Tahquitz rocks were world-famous. San Diego County had a lot of climbable rocks, but they weren't high enough to attract much attention from outsiders. Yosemite was a full day's drive away. When Stonemaster Ron Kauk wore a bandana he looked like an Apache warrior. When George Manson wore one, he looked like he belonged to a motorcycle gang. The Stonemasters were rumoured to take psychedelic drugs. George and his friends liked beer well enough to name the first 5.10 at Rattlesnake Molson.

George was a Canadian cousin who joined Tom and Greg's summer adventures. He drove a delivery truck in Toronto during the winter and stayed fit for Yosemite by revolutionizing Rattlesnake climbing. George had brought the 5.10 standard to the area and followed it up by climbing many of the first climbs at the 5.11 standard established by Mike Tschipper and Rob Rohn. George's friends found him charismatic, and Tom followed him to Toronto and lived there for several years. Greg also visited, making a few hard first ascents. When they weren't at Rattlesnake, the group climbed in the Shawangunk, Adirondack and White Mountains, and at Bon Echo. At Rattlesnake and Bon Echo, there was something seigneurial about them, as if they owned the place. They were the first people I had met who rock climbed as a way of life. George seemed to be the leader, and although he had a job and a wife, he seemed to not give a shit about anything that day as he climbed steadily and silently in his aviator shades and biker bandana.

Dave Lanman climbed next, splaying himself under the roof, swearing and blindly groping for a handhold. He grimaced as his toes hooked behind a flake. A lunge for the cigarette-pack hold left his legs dangling in the air. Then he put his foot on a hold by his waist, pulled on a little crack and stood above the overhang whooping in victory. All I knew about Dave at the time was that he came from suburbia like me and had learned from more experienced partners. It was enough. I believed that with effort, I could do what he was doing.

William's desire to climb waned after we discovered Rattlesnake Point. When I asked him to climb he usually had other things to do. A game we had played on our own, partly because we didn't fit in at school, had become something serious for me, but not for him.

We climbed together only a few more times. I began to be embarrassed by our foolhardy beginnings and even to sometimes deny or omit them when I discussed climbing with others. William reacted by taking climbing less seriously than ever and ignoring the little we knew about safety. For his younger brother's first rock climb, he picked a route with long traverses so that even with a top-rope, a fall would swing him across the cliff face. As Ian approached a difficult overhang, he shouted that he wanted to go down. He was afraid William would drop him if he fell.

William said he wouldn't. That would be stupid. Ian

reached up with a whimper, his hiking boots skated and he fell. Twenty feet below, he landed upright on a flat slab. He howled in pain, untied and punched William in the head. I had brought Reg to show that I had become a real climber, but he sat there silently and I knew he saw me as a fool. It would be more than a year before he would come back.

In the evening of the last day of Grade 10, William and I sat in the big catalpa tree in his front yard, drinking his mother's beer. He was putting on weight and shedding the slightly starved look he had always had when we were kids. He recounted how, on a camping trip, he had woken Ian by putting his clothes on the fire and filling his tent with the smoke, and the next morning Ian got his revenge by burning William's boots. But the story didn't make me laugh. I had just been on a climbing trip to the Adirondacks and said we should go back to Bon Echo and try to get things right, but William didn't have time. He said he was training for tryouts for the football team.

My summer job helping a climbing camp instructor ended when he quit halfway through the season. Unqualified to run the program, I was soon on the bus to the city as well. My mother and sisters were in Mexico with my father. Reg was in Timmins, in northern Ontario, working as a junior forest ranger, helping out with trail maintenance, forest fire prevention and beer drinking. I arrived back at the hot, empty house on Islington Avenue in late July.

I lived off whatever cans and boxes of instant food were left in the cupboards. Television offered a little relief from nightly ennui, but it was before video cassette rental, so I had to watch whatever the local networks broadcast. The best movie on TV that summer was *The Eiger Sanction*, starring Clint Eastwood as Jonathan Hemlock, an alpinist, assassin and art collector. The scenes filmed with climbers as doubles on the actual north face of the Eiger amazed me. Canadian climber Chic Scott, who helped film the climbing, later told me that the scenes were so realistic that a climber on the crew was killed. The sex scenes, with blaxploitation actress Vonetta McGee, were less well-lit. My favourite character was an American Native climbing instructor and seductress played by 18-year-old Brenda Venus. Venus was also a muse of aging erotic writer Henry Miller, a favourite author of many climbers. Miller spent several years wishing that, like Jonathan, he could sleep with Venus, but he never did.

That summer, a magazine that tried to make climbing as urbane as Eastwood's Hemlock hit the newsstands. *Outside* covered climbing, mountaineering and other adventure sports and was glossy and commercial. *Mountain's* insider gossip and esoteric photos made climbers look sectarian and elitist. *Outside* made outdoor athletes into sexy celebrities and implied that outdoor adventure had broad appeal. I read both magazines.

Climbing's popularity increased the crowds at Rattlesnake, to my advantage. Although I had less than $50 to live off for that whole month, I climbed every day. I rode my bike to Highway 401, hid it in the bushes and hitchhiked out to a trailhead where I walked to the cliff along the Bruce Trail. There were always at least a couple of climbers there to belay me, even though I often overreached myself and fell.

My partners were mainly graduates of adult outdoor education programs. Even if I could have afforded to take these courses, I was too young to enjoy their singles-night atmosphere, and their emphasis on safety seemed unexciting. Fortunately, before my ignorance had serious consequences, I got to climb with savvy men who I saw as fully realized adults, although they were rarely more than a few years older than me.

Typical of my efforts of the time was an attempt on an overhanging corner on Rattlesnake's East Cliff. My arms ached and I felt dizzy at the final overhang. The overhang was two grades harder than what I had already done, but I often acted as if the normal standards simply didn't apply to me. I quickly climbed down, my feet shaking with the strain on my ankles as my toes gripped the small ledges. I just made it to the last piece of protection when I fell off. The nut tore out and I saved myself from a ground fall by jumping into a nearby tree. Norbert, with whom I had climbed Sweet Dreams at Bon Echo, finished the climb easily, and I followed him, falling on top-rope twice where I would have hit the ground if I had been leading. When he said it was good that I had finally learned to respect the grade system, he gave me too much credit.

Paradoxically, the three men who helped me most in my quest to become a real lead climber ran a school that trained scores of top-ropers. Given how much of my attention I diverted from school into climbing, it was also a little ironic that two were school teachers.

Brian Hibbert was a school principal nicknamed the Field Marshal because of his resemblance to Bernard Montgomery, although I suspect the moustache that contributed to the look was inspired by English climbing hotshot Ron Fawcett and not the victor of El Alamein. He had learned to climb in the United Kingdom and had a photograph of himself on North Wales's Cenotaph Corner, a climb I had seen in *Hard Rock*. He lived up to his nickname by encouraging his students to "bash on regardless," and if they hung on a rope to rest, cursing them with the names of non-existent gods and suggesting they perform impossible acts. They loved him.

His friend, Dave Moore, a high-school physical education teacher, ran the school with him. He knew every hold on the cliff, and his school-team coaching style was a good counterpoint to Brian's Britishisms. Rick Clark, the third partner, had a massive upper body and a calm, childlike demeanour, two attributes that made him an excellent ice climber. He worked as a pipefitter and had a small family and a house in a subdivision.

The 30 or so students enjoyed the courses so much that many of them enrolled year after year, but even those who didn't enrol benefitted from their instructors' generosity. I met Brian and David when they let me climb on the ropes they set up for their students. That same day, after many falls, I seconded Brian on Funky Fingers, my first 5.11. Over the coming years, Brian, Rick and David drove me to the cliff, loaned me gear and gave me advice that probably saved my life and definitely made me a better climber.

I also learned things that weren't on their photocopied course syllabus.

On the way to the cliff, Brian, wearing a shirt declaring himself a sex instructor offering the first lesson free, was a bleary raconteur of the previous night's adventures, which usually involved cocktails and charming his way out of scrapes of all kinds. After climbing, the trio decamped to a pub in Milton. Rick was quiet, but Brian and David flirted with women and drank Rusty Nails. David was a master of the dirty joke in its traditional long form. Brian recounted epics from his climbing trips and the antics of his semi-feral husky dog and speculated about where his missing pet boa constrictor had gone or whether a climber with an earring was a homosexual.

Brian Hibbert, Dave Moore and Rick Clark were pivotal

in the creation of the Ontario Rock Climbing Association (ORCA), which introduced standards for climbing instruction to the province after a couple of fatal climbing accidents. If you thought that the regular crowd at Rattlesnake was strange, ORCA's lost tribes were a revelation. There were those who tried to make up for a lack of climbing talent with a knack for teaching, and those more like me, who had no teaching ability but hoped to make a few bucks. Little climbing clans came from towns all over Ontario, where they had used magazines and mail-order books to teach themselves climbing at local lover's leaps and road cuts.

The largest of these groups came from Kingston and was founded by Rob Chisnall. He was an expert on knots who travelled the world to testify at ligature murders. Pioneering new routes at cliffs few others had seen and traversing the walls of Queen's University kept him in excellent shape. He held the Guinness World Record for one-hand and one-finger pull-ups and was rumoured to be an expert martial artist.

Rob introduced us to Peter Arbic, who everyone called P.A., a climber who had joined the back-to-the-land movement and bought a cheap farm north of Kingston. Although he was about 20, his army surplus climbing pants, Che Guevara beard and round, wire-rimmed glasses made him seem older than he really was. After meeting him at Rattlesnake, we often ran into him ice climbing on the Canadian Shield or cragging in the Shawangunks. P.A. and some friends started a short-lived outdoor gear co-operative. The last night we climbed with him, we snuck into a small-town laundromat to avoid the sub-zero nighttime temperatures and shared a bottle of cheap rum. Even then, there was something intense and coiled about him, beneath his laid-back demeanour. None of us could have guessed, however, that within a few seasons, P.A. would give up his hippie lifestyle, climb some of the hardest routes in the Rockies and the Alps, make a wild attempt on Nanga Parbat and complete hundreds of new rock routes.

All these men were legends in my world. They did innumerable favours for me, and I cannot think of a single criticism against them, but as a young man, I longed not only for mentors but also for my own tribe.

This was on my mind one morning as I watched Dave Lanman, who I had once watched on Space Case, climbing back and forth across the low overhang by the spring at Rattlesnake Point. Although I had never climbed with him, since he was clearly more skilled than me, I saw him at the cliff often, and we knew each other by name.

Dave jumped down and stuffed a spent cigarette in a pocket in the rock. The stripes of his sweater were stretched tight across his ribcage. His forearms and hands, the first things climbers look at when they meet, were like mallets. He had cut his hair since I had seen him on Space Case. His eyes were serious, but he liked to smile. A girl belaying a man on Crepidation, the difficult climb above the spring, had been staring at the gingham patch on the seat of Dave's white pants. He asked her for a smoke.

Letting go of the belay rope as the climber struggled at an overhang, she rummaged in her pockets for a pack of cigarettes. Dave took one and she lit it for him. The leader shouted to her to pay attention.

"Dude, you should relax." Dave told him, and thanked the girl.

She picked up the rope and swore at the leader, whose legs were so tremulous I was sure he would fall. Dave looked at me conspiratorially. If the climber had fallen when she was lighting the cigarette, he might have been killed. Dropping the belay rope was high in the serious sins against safety – maybe at the top of the list – but I smiled back.

I never saw women climb with George Manson and his friends. George's wife didn't share his hobby, and it was as difficult to see him answering to a wife or anyone else as it was to imagine him without his climbing equipment. He seemed to live through winters at home so he could make money to spend the summer months on the road, climbing. The young men he shared this life with were mainly too Spartan in their detachment from the pleasures of the world to join Brian Hibbert at the pub. Too young for bars, Dave Lanman revelled in joints at the cliff and bottles of cheap red in paper bags in the boat at Bon Echo. Hedonistic and spontaneous, he happily accepted that spending time with his girlfriend kept him on the margin of George's group. The joyous, disordered mood of his climbing was infectious.

Dave had heard I wanted to do hard climbs and asked if I wanted to do one with him. Part of me held back, having seen him on Space Case. What, exactly, had he heard? Not long before, I'd been using a rack from a hardware store and considered wearing an army helmet on a shale outcrop. My climbing partner had almost died falling a few feet from an underpass and quit to try out for the high-school football team.

He suggested a 5.10 close by. I admitted I had never climbed at that grade, but Dave ignored me and explained how to do the climb. He even offered to climb it and show me how it was done, but I declined in case he used some intimidating advanced manoeuvre that made it look even harder than it was. Dave belayed with one hand, smoked with the other and winked at a girl instead of watching me. It should have made me feel unsafe, but it had the opposite effect. William's haphazard belaying made me nervous, but Dave's bad belaying inspired me. I believed that he was only doing it because he thought I was too cool to fall off the Mother.

The crux was a strange move on a small pocket. The bolt was below me, but it was old and stuck out too far to be secure. I was at the limit of my ability to hold on. A small error in the angle of my foot would pitch me off the rock face, but I was able to avoid that error long enough to get to bigger holds above.

Dave showed me how to descend from the ledge by stepping into a tree and climbing down its branches to the spring. We would spend hours climbing variations to the climbs ending at that ledge and use every handhold on the steep wall, partly because of how easy it was to swing down the tree. Soon, however, the tree began growing away from the cliff, and we had to start jumping for it. A few seasons later, most of us left the cliff for several years. When I came back, the tree had grown beyond reach and the chalk marks and memories of all those variations had faded.

The climbs I was doing were long established, but George and his friends tackled much harder ones in the same area that summer. Fearless Warrior, a thin crack in a wall of leaning white rock at Cow Crag, was difficult to protect, with its first piece of protection 30 feet off the ground. Return of the Degnoid at Punk Rock was a finger-width crack splitting two overhangs and one of the hardest short climbs in Canada. It is still seldom climbed.

September 1978 came, and the maples and oaks below the cliffs reddened. My idyll at Rattlesnake ended as my parents returned and school resumed. I savoured the last days on the rock – there were no indoor climbing gyms in the 1970s, and the cliffs and most of my climbing partners wouldn't be seen again until spring.

By then, I knew George just well enough to ask for a lift home at the end of the day. Where Brian Hibbert swerved left for the pub, George Manson went right, down the winding road below the escarpment, through the fields of hay ricks and the orchards where the harvest had begun. He pulled up to a small cliff-band next to a chalky road. His pickup truck sputtered to silence and the dust settled on the hood. He put on his climbing shoes and started zigzagging up and down the cliff face without touching the ground. I tried to do the same, but had only made it up and down a few times before George reached the end of the cliff. I tried to keep climbing, although I had already had a full day at Rattlesnake, and my arms were tired and my fingertips raw.

Back on the highway, he asked whether I knew Picnic Butt, as Dave was sometimes called because of the gingham patch on his climbing pants. He spoke about a trip they had made to Bon Echo. Dave had pointed to a photo of the Rockies on the hut wall and asked what the white stuff on top of the mountains was. When George had said it was angel shit, there was an argument with a climber who accused George of bringing random kids climbing who didn't care about traditions. George seemed amused by the anecdote and the climb he and Dave had done that weekend.

"I go up, try it, it's maybe 5.10; crap protection," he said. "I climb down so I don't weight the rope and rip out the protection. Picnic Butt says, 'Relax,' takes the hammer and drill, goes past my highpoint and does a few hard moves. He starts hammering and throwing off loose rock. So far, there's maybe only one piece of good protection. Suddenly he says, 'Lower me, express!' At the belay, he swears he lowered off something bombproof. I go up, try the crux, fall a couple of times. I finally get to the anchor, and it's a rivet. A quarter inch of cheesy aluminum between me and..." He gnawed on an apple. His expression might have been a smile or a sneer.

"Know what I'm gonna call that route?" he asked. "Fool's End."

CHAPTER 4

To Chapel Pond

O n a nondescript afternoon at SEE in October 1977, I put
down my pen and gave up writing about a book I hadn't
read. I followed voices to a room where a youth in a top hat
recited *The Waste Land*, part of the syllabus of Grade 13
English. His friends listened in stoned adoration.

In the corner, Judy Paddon sat at a desk, ignoring him,
staring through oversized glasses at a textbook and writing
furiously in a binder. I told her I remembered her and her dog
from grade school, and she looked up. I had seen her at SEE before but hadn't introduced myself. Judy looked at me for a few
seconds. She was tiny, with long brown braids held up with
tortoiseshell combs. After pulling on a French ski jacket she
gathered her books.

We took the bus to the Royal York subway station, not far
from where I lived in Etobicoke, and I walked home with her,

without really knowing whether she wanted me to. She loved to talk. She was a year ahead of me. She wanted to go to university, her parents wanted her to, her marks were good, she liked science. Her father was a lawyer. There were family ski holidays in Quebec and the Rockies and a cottage in Muskoka. She and her friend, Bea, who also went to SEE, were competitive swimmers. Judy hated *Some Girls*, a recent Rolling Stones album, she had never been drunk, her sister wanted to be a model, her brother was a brat. Judy had strong feelings and big ideas.

We talked about the books we read in English. She admired the political and social messages of *A Clockwork Orange, Catch-22* and *Journey to Ixtlan*. The deep implications of the books were lost on me, but their protagonists seemed like the kind of guys who would skip homework for long runs and workouts and hitchhike to the cliffs.

The freedom of SEE was a boon for self-motivated students like Judy or genius misfits like Adam Sobolak. Teachers had confused his awkwardness for an intellectual disability. At SEE, however, he got top grades and wrote an analysis of the pop music radio playlists and sold it to a local radio station. He later became an art historian.

Although I read all the books and my writing improved a little, my assignments were always late or incomplete because I climbed when I was meant to be studying. Judy was the opposite. When I asked her to go to the movie based on

Hermann Hesse's *Steppenwolf* at the Kingsway repertory theatre, she agreed, but only because she was studying the novel. The movie was even more confusing than the book, but Max von Sydow's sad middle-aged Harry made growing up seem satisfyingly pointless.

I tried to talk to her about climbing, but it felt awkward, like I was entrusting her with a secret. She surprised me, however, by asking me to take her to the cliffs.

We stopped near her house, where we could see the steeple of the church we had both attended as children. She told me that she used to take a forbidden shortcut through the cemetery on the way to school. She justified it by knowing that she was going to apologize as soon as she got to school and everyone recited the Lord's Prayer.

I leaned down, and instead of turning away she raised her chin, looking solemn and rebellious. She crushed me into her down-filled ski jacket. There were aromas of pool chlorine, perfume and tobacco in her hair. She released her grip and we kissed.

A week later, we were driving down the middle of Highway 401 at 40 miles an hour, the top speed of the 1967 Volkswagen Beetle her father had given her for her 16th birthday. Trucks honked and tried to force us out of the passing lane. Cars travelling at the speed limit seemed to race past. Judy always drove slower than the limit and in the middle lane so she could turn left or right if she needed to.

In the back seat, Bea, skinny and blue-eyed with blonde hair tinged green by pool chlorine, tapped her toes to the Foreigner song playing on the radio. William Jack sat beside her and explained that he had failed football tryouts because of how much time he spent climbing. He offered to climb with her that day. She declined.

No one else was at Kelso on that late-fall day. William took Judy to an awkward climb up a wide crack. Instead of just climbing it, he decided to make a hanging belay above some grassy ledges 20 feet up. Whether he was buying time to delay leading or trying to show his technical wizardry, his only anchor was a nut a little thicker than a nickel and it ripped out as soon as they hung on it. They both rolled down the hill, but neither of them was hurt.

William often struggled with safety equipment. Usually I had ignored these legacies of our days playing at climbers, even though they were dangerous. Now that I was climbing with real rock climbers, though, seeming inexpert was embarrassing. It wasn't really about safety; I still couldn't imagine a real accident happening to me or anyone I knew. When I rebuked William in front of the girls for the bad anchor, I saw resignation in his eyes. The episode decreased his already declining enthusiasm for climbing and confirmed my sense that he would never take it seriously enough for me.

While William and Judy struggled in their chimney, I wriggled up a vertical crack in the quarry, throwing out chunks of rock and wondering if anyone had climbed it before. The climbing was easy, but using the back on one side of the chimney and feet and hands on the other was difficult for Bea. She struggled and screamed like an animal caught in a trap and hung on the rope to rest but refused to quit. At the top, she was breathing heavily and her hair was stringy with sweat. I had expected her to be angry, but she thanked me. I don't know whether she ever climbed again.

In the weakening late afternoon light, Judy and I climbed Corner Route, a giant's staircase on the cliff's prow. She held my hand as we hiked down to our packs.

A week later, Judy, Bea and I were at a movie at the Kingsway Theatre. During a musical number, Judy dragged Bea into the aisle to dance with the rest of the kids. When the song ended, they fell to the floor, as if dead. After the show, Judy and I listened to music and made out in her basement while her mother drank martinis in the living room.

Bea lived in a bungalow in northern Etobicoke. She shared her family's obsession with hockey, but she was also obsessed with Bach's keyboard concertos. One day, while she played the Prelude and Fugue No. 5 in D Major, I unbuttoned her blouse. Her mother came home and she increased her tempo as I quickly re-buttoned it. When she came to the end, she closed the key cover.

"I was just practicing," she said. "David's leaving."

A few weeks later she said she wanted to be a concert

pianist and that my climbing bored her. "Why not play hockey if you're going to do a sport?" she asked. As a farewell present, she he gave me a copy of Tagore's *Gitanjali*, inscribed: "With love, Bea." Why did no one see that my whole point was that climbing wasn't a sport, or at least not a sport like hockey? Bea went to another school. Certain phrases from Tagore or Bach still remind me of her, but I never saw her again.

Of course I never took Bea's advice about hockey, but that winter I did find myself on ice. Ice climbing was new but grew quickly in Canada, where winters were long and the Canadian Rockies had more frozen waterfalls than anywhere else in the world. Ontario climbers made do with the single-rope-length icicles of the Canadian Shield or the cliffs of Hamilton, where some of the falls flowed from storm drains.

Specialized gear requirements made ice climbing more complicated than rock climbing. There were crampons, warm boots and ice axes, and hammers with curved picks that stuck in the ice with a reassuring thunk, although they were hard to pull out. Ice screws were about as secure as modern ones, but much harder to place, even with a bolt ratchet modified to torque them in.

Ice climbing attracted climbers I'd never met at rock cliffs. Henry worked in an army surplus and hunting store that sold a few pieces of climbing hardware. When Brian Hibbert pulled up to Henry's basement apartment before dawn, the lights were always out. I stood in the cold, pounding the door until he awoke, then waited as he scoured piles of camping and fishing gear and a broom closet full of guns for his climbing gear. One morning, instead of coming to the door, he shouted that I should go away. He had leapt out of bed onto his crampons. There was a lot of blood.

Henry pushed himself on the ice, but he was unfit. Wrecked from the effort of one climb, he rushed into a yard backing onto the cliff and defecated. The homeowner saw him and phoned the police, who called us down from the cliff with a loud-hailer and shooed us off.

Ice climbing was good practice for alpinism because, like mountains, waterfalls were more dangerous than crags, and mountains tended to be icy. Although equipment could make rock climbing safe, it merely made ice climbing possible. Barbed steel crampons and ice tool blades could cut you or the rope, even if you didn't fall. Although ice screws seemed more likely to fail than rock protection, nobody I knew had been brave or foolish enough to fall on one. The ice itself was always breaking free, both from the impact of ice tools and from changes in temperature.

Brian Hibbert was the contact for mountaineers stranded in Toronto looking for ice. Through him, I met Jim Elzinga, a huge Albertan who climbed steep ice with ease. He and his usual climbing partner, John Lauchlan, were Canadian mountaineering stars. They had made the first ascents of two-thousand-foot-high waterfalls in the Canadian Rockies and suffered for days on new routes in Yukon's Saint Elias Range. They wanted to be the first Canadians on the summit of Mount Everest, which was still infrequently climbed. Jim was trying to stay in shape for climbing while making a living as a photographer in Toronto. He seemed as glamorous as the climbers in Bonington's books.

Although frozen waterfalls offered a way to climb in the winter, I looked forward to the Alpine Club–sponsored slideshows almost as much. Even the usual program of slides of climbers trudging up low-angled peaks in the Canadian Rockies, with its geography-class discourse on peak heights, topography and geology, was more interesting than a night at home. Occasionally, however, the show would be about rock climbing and the minutiae of grades and types of rock climbs, which fascinated me. That winter, Rob Rohn, who had made the first free ascent of Space Case, partnered with George Manson and Tom Gibson to present slides of Western rock climbing.

The climbers were specks against silver walls. Hands covered in athletic tape to prevent pressure cuts were jammed in cracks splitting clean walls. Racks of pitons as varied as pots in a bazaar hung from the shoulders of big-wall climbers. Starry nights on ledgeless walls were spent in tiny hammocks, and the sun shone on ten-storey-high sequoias so far below that they looked like they were decorating a toy railway. At the end of the show, Rob, George and Tom threw in some slides of Cow Crag and Punk Rock, hard little cliffs near Milton they had found and named. Some of the routes were on steep, smooth walls; others climbed cracks in big over-hangs. Showing these little treasures at this point in the slide-show gave the impression that being skilled enough to climb them – which, as yet, I was not – would bring me closer to my big-wall dreams.

That night, the big wall ceased to be a fairy-tale castle in books and became a test I set for myself. From then until I passed that test, I believed that it would prove my stature in every possible way. I feared failing at this more than an-ything else. I was already floundering at school, losing my parents' approval and finding girls inscrutable, but none of these setbacks would matter to me if I succeeded in my cho-sen goal.

After the show, Brian Hibbert and other climbers old enough to drink discussed which bar they would go to. I stared at a poster of the Lotus Flower Tower in the Northwest Territories. The crack to its summit was so thin, continuous and plumb-line perfect that it looked like it had been sliced in the two-thousand-foot-high nose of stone with a giant razor.

I met Mike Tschipper, a boy my age with an unusually normal haircut for a climber, a pair of corduroys and an em-broidered sweater that made him look like he had dressed for Oktoberfest. He had deep-set, intense eyes. "It's maybe 15 pitches. Only half of El Cap. But it's all free, up to 5.10. It's only been done free once," he said. I was really impressed. My longest routes had been tiny by comparison.

I later learned that Mike's parents had introduced him to climbing in the Alps. In Canada they took him to Rattlesnake, the local *klettergarten*, as German climbers called crags where alpinists trained for the mountains. He met Rob, George and Tom, and since there were no mountains to practice for, climbed rocks for their own sake.

Mike was unlucky. A 90-foot fall from a difficult route at Bon Echo broke his leg, and he was pulled up the cliff on a rope, weeping with frustration and pain. A year later, he made a free ascent of the Lotus Flower Tower with George, Rob, Tom, Mike and a local climber named Sean Lewis. They made the cover of an outdoor magazine. The other climbers looked happy and relieved to be on the summit, but Mike squinted and frowned a little.

Then Mike almost succeeded on Mescalito, one of the hardest climbs on El Capitan at the time, but two thousand feet up, he was leading a crack on a slender pillar called the Bismarck when he tore off a loose rock and fell to a ledge, breaking an arm. He was plucked from the face by a helicopter in a terrifying rescue.

After a winter recovering at his parents' house in Thornhill, a suburb north of Toronto, he was back in Yosemite. He appeared sullen and indifferent. He joked about violence. There was a short stint in the Yosemite jail. He borrowed equipment for long climbs but was surprised that anyone trusted him enough to expect its return.

Hanging out and climbing on the 1,500-foot granite walls of Squamish, British Columbia, he took some LSD. The bad trip broke him. A decade later, he called Reg a few times from pay phones, agitated, wanting to talk about his climbing days. His family eventually found a place where he was cared for, a long way from the cliffs and mountains. I think he is still there.

After the rock-climbing slideshow, Dave Lanman, who had had a minor grudge against the Alpine Club ever since its minimum age requirement had prevented him from going with Steven to Bon Echo, decided we should try a club meeting anyway. Enthusiasm for my new hobby overcame the shyness that had previously stopped me from joining clubs, and I went too.

The meeting convened in a sitting room in a big Edwardian house. Bearded men with ice-axe pins in their lapels sat beneath a painting of an alpine lake. An elderly woman offered us tea and showed us a poem in a book she held reverently, asking me if I had read it. I started mid-stanza. It was about a goat falling to its death in the Canadian Rockies. Dave giggled.

The meeting was chaired by Jim Mark, the guidebook author. With his trim beard, fine manners and modest height, he was just as I had imagined him. A discussion about repairing the dock and boat at Bon Echo gave way to a call for proposals of locations for something called a general mountaineering camp. Robert's Rules made these discussions seem interminable. I felt a little like I was visiting a rich relative's yacht club on Toronto Island. I hoped no one would ask me a question, in case I mispronounced Maligne Lake or Tonquin Valley.

Although Dave and I weren't what British officers in war movies called "clubbable," we agreed with the club's unstated position that climbers were superior beings. The members' love of the Rockies mirrored and gave credence to the intense feelings we had for our own native rocks. In the long run, we both benefitted tremendously from the club's existence.

When spring of 1978 came, the warm rock fulfilled the promise of a winter of looking at pictures of climbing and talking about it. Judy climbed with me often, and we planned an early summer trip to the Adirondack Mountains, a hundred miles south of Montreal. Some of the climbs there were seven hundred feet long, more than twice the length of the routes at Bon Echo.

The Volkswagen was rusting badly and had no gas gauge, so Judy's father declared it unworthy of a long trip. We took the all-night bus to Montreal, where we slouched on benches with the drug addicts and loners until a bus took us to Lake Placid, stopping in a dozen small towns along the way. At the border, we showed our money and emptied our climbing equipment onto the pavement.

"It's a privilege to be allowed into the United States. Don't see any boat people in this stuff," said the border patrolman, fingering my climbing gear suspiciously and sizing up Judy. "I take it you ain't his mother?" he said, and waved us on.

I had imagined Lake Placid as the kind of rustic mountain town I had seen in old books about the Alps. Even with the alpine souvenir shops, boutiques and ski stores closed, however, the speakers from a closed tea shop piping accordion music onto the empty sidewalk made it feel like an abandoned carnival midway. We were tired and hungry but walked straight out of town to hitchhike to Keene Valley.

A day after leaving Toronto, we jumped off the bed of a pickup truck onto the floor of a valley of dark green forests walled with grey granite cliffs. We tossed our sleeping bags beneath one of the boulders in the forest below the great sweep of Chapel Pond Slab. The sky darkened, and by dinnertime a curtain of rain had descended.

Two young Americans joined us that night. Tad, who had dark, stringy hair, later became a climbing ranger in American national parks. Fred was tall and thin, with a ponytail that made him look like he had climbed in California, which, as I found out, he had. We read and talked and tried to make tea on a fire of damp sticks. The cave filled with smoke from the joints Fred rolled from a plastic bag of what he called Jersey Red. They told stories about their usual climbing area, the Shawangunks. The Gunks, as climbers knew the area, had steep three-hundred-foot-high cliffs with lots of overhangs. New Paltz, the town below, was full of students, climbers and weirdoes.

Judy was stoned. "Sounds wonderful," she said, "maybe it isn't raining there."

When the rain stopped, we climbed a route on the left side of Chapel Pond Slab, a featureless but low-angled ramp of stone like the Californian ones I had seen in Royal Robbins's books. There were few cracks, but the angle was easy and the rock warm and rough. Judy padded up the grey incline as I took in the rope.

Looking down I saw girl rock, and wilderness: a trinity of all that mattered. At the belay I wanted to say something about what I felt, but I didn't know how. There's a photo of me racking my carabiners on a sling and trying to look serious.

In five rope-lengths we reached the top. A black cloud rolled over the mountain, extinguishing the sun and releasing a deluge of rain. The rappel gully streamed with water, pine needles and small stones, tangling the rope in low pine branches. At the bottom, I tried to untangle the rope with numb fingers while Judy shivered. I gave up and carried it in a pile.

Underneath our boulder, we crawled into our sleeping bags until the next morning, when sunlight shone through the steaming trees. We checked the road for cars and crossed furtively. The pines were damp and fragrant as we hiked to the vertical cliffs of the Upper Washbowl.

The crux of our climb was a crack in a corner made by two walls near the clifftop. I climbed it quickly but clumsily, since the layback movement it demanded was unfamiliar to me. It was also scary, because my poor technique made it hard to see inside the crack to place protection. Judy climbed slowly and thoughtfully, bridging the two walls with her legs to rest every few feet on footholds I had missed.

Fred and Tad had hitchhiked south, leaving a joint and a note saying they'd see us in the Gunks sometime. Judy pocketed the note and we smoked the joint. After we made out and had an argument, I sat alone watching the shadows of the mountains darken the water of Chapel Pond until night came.

In the morning we hitchhiked back to Lake Placid and the long bus ride home. Ahead of me lay my short career teaching climbing at a camp, and my long summer at Rattlesnake on my own.

Judy went to Outward Bound in British Columbia. One of her instructors was a Gunks climber. He knew George and Rob and had made the first ascent of a route at Rattlesnake named Crack-Up after the tiny metal hook he used to protect it. She told him about how she started climbing. He said she was lucky to have survived and I was likely to kill myself one of these days because I didn't know what I was doing.

He was only partly right. As the climbing season of 1978 came to an end, I knew my quest to become myself through climbing the imperfect climbs within my reach might kill me.

Anyone with a few years of climbing could measure the gaps in my knowledge. I had climbed just barely enough to be able to measure them too.

I still have a photo Judy took that fall, after she came home. The angle is downhill and oblique. My long hair is tucked under a headband, and carabiners and nuts hang on a sling decorated with a scrap of embroidery. My hands are small, my fingers a little delicate. My 16-year-old's stubble makes me look like a beggar. I seem to stare at both rock and photographer with a hunger for impossible things.

CHAPTER 5

Little Spiders

R eg and I were two years apart, so we grew up with differ-ent teachers and friends. It was only when we were teen-agers that our interests and social circles converged. Reg was handsome and popular but struggled in class and fought in the playground. Although tests showed he was smart, adults inter-preted his difficulties with reading and his schoolyard scraps as signs that he was anti-social. Their disapproval frustrated him and quickened his temper. Adult punishments, however, made him a hero to other kids, since his victims were always bullies.

My mother was usually home when the principal's of-fice phoned to complain that Reg was faltering at school. She knew how hard it was to escape misfortune without an educa-tion, perhaps because she had done so herself. It disappointed my father that Reg preferred the fields of McGillivray's Hill to school, and the drafty old farmhouse to a home where there were books, classical music and precisely timed meals. Reg was sent first to a tutor and then to a private school. His marks improved and he fought less, but the school only went to Grade 8, and afterwards, at his own request, he went to a public high school.

His marks sunk again. In remedial classes he made new friends but learned more about partying and rock and roll than history and math. A season as a junior forest ranger offered opportunities to use his new knowledge and revived his love of the wilderness but decreased his enthusiasm for school. When he dropped out, the school was relieved and my parents weren't surprised. My grandfather assumed that his own good sense had skipped a generation and got Reg a job sorting packages for a printing house. The minimum wage paid for a small apartment, where Reg and his friends played his stereo, smoked and drank beer.

Some winter weekends they clattered down Collingwood's icy hills on rented skis and vomited their beer on the ski-lifts. None of Reg's friends knew that from those hills Reg saw, and remembered, the woods he had roamed as a child. When he didn't have bus money, he skied alone through the golf courses and ravines running north from the city to woodlots and river valleys that were disappearing beneath shopping malls and subdivisions. Snow squalls sometimes hid the apartment buildings and high-tension wires and made the white-treed parks look like a wilderness.

A survival camping course offered Reg a reunion with the backcountry. The instructor had sinister, paramilitary credentials, but his little band was armed only with knives tucked in their high-top Greb boots. Reg loved the hungry weekends avoiding cottages, making lean-tos and stalking rodents. His fragile, premature compromise with the city of adults eroded.

Sometime around midnight on New Year's Eve, 1977, Reg passed out in the midst of a party and the wheel of his life, which had been temporarily halted, turned. At dawn on the first day of 1978, he woke to find most of his furniture destroyed and his old friends gone. An eviction notice had been pushed under the door. I helped him and my father pack plastic milk boxes full of vinyl records and wide-collar shirts and took crates of empty bottles, shot glasses and bongs to the dumpster.

Katimavik was a new nine-month government program for young people from across Canada. Its name means "meeting place" in Inuktitut, the Inuit language. Room and board were free, and participants who stayed until the end were given a $1,000 cheque. Reg's options appeared to be diminishing, so he signed up, spending three months apiece in Whitehorse, Yukon; Estevan, Saskatchewan; and Jonquière, Québec.

When he was done, he came home with back-to-the-land philosophies, eight-track tapes of Cat Stevens, a ponytail that kept falling out of his too-short hair and a tiny girlfriend from Quebec who spoke little English. He was still dangerous, even as a hippie. Driving slowly where he had drag raced less than a year before, he braked for an old lady. Another driver swerved to avoid a rear-end collision and almost killed her.

A few weeks later, the girlfriend left, taking Cat and the bad driving with her. His brief hippie days over, Reg enrolled in a course in food preparation at a community college. His Katimavik honorarium got him a white, 1971, AMC Hornet at a scrapyard under the cloverleaf overpass by Six Points Plaza in central Etobicoke. It was small, but it had a big v8 engine. He said it was the fastest car you could buy for less than a grand.

For years it ran beautifully, despite amateur roadside repairs. We nicknamed it Millennium Falcon, after Han Solo's decrepit spaceship in *Star Wars*. It survived a dozen transcontinental climbing trips before Reg finally stripped the plates off its corroded frame and left it on a Calgary street.

Reg was happy to use his car on the weekends to escape the drudgery of his job as a diner cook. He invited me on a backpacking trip on the Bruce Trail, partly because I was one of the few people he knew who was interested in the outdoors. That weekend, we spent more time together than we had since we were children. As we hiked, he spoke about how hurt he had been by the sale of McGillivray's Hill. It seemed like a loss he would never recoup. I didn't know what to say and was quiet until the trail came up against a rock wall.

"I climb stuff like this." I said, changing the subject. Reg looked skeptical, undoubtedly remembering when William Jack dropped his brother Ian off Rattlesnake to teach him a lesson. I assured him I had improved since then and asked him to come climbing with me.

"If you were worse," he said, "you'd be dead."

The motive of my invitation was partly selfish. Judy's Volkswagen had been sold for scrap. She had moved a few miles away to a mansion with a spiral staircase and a fountain in the foyer. We spoke on the phone more than we saw each other, and we only met in person when we climbed. We quarrelled often, not because she didn't want to climb, but because it seemed like it was all I wanted.

A few months after our backpacking trip, Reg said he wanted to climb. I welcomed his interest, because I suspected that unlike Judy, Reg wouldn't ruin climbing days by asking whether I had aspirations outside of climbing. Reg and I first climbed together on a blue-sky day in October 1978, the month of his 18th birthday. For his debut, I chose Pinocchio, which was halfway up the scale of difficulty, at 5.6. I had done it many times, mastering the crux, where I stuck my fingers in holes in the rock face that were invisible from below. It was a poor choice for a beginner, but it would show him that I was now a proper climber.

Steve Labelle was already climbing the route. In Yosemite he had been hit by a paper bag full of shit thrown from a bivouac ledge on El Capitan, earning him the nickname Shitty. Self-deprecating and honest, he realized that even without the shit bag, the giant walls and hardest climbs weren't for him. After he returned from Yosemite, he usually either top-roped or did easy climbs. On his rare leads, a cigarette hung from his lips to help him relax. He placed a lot of protection and moved slowly, without interrupting his chain-smoking. He didn't cheat death for long, however. A cancer unrelated to smoking killed him when he was still a young man.

Steve was seconded by Bryan, who was wearing a T-shirt proclaiming that he'd "rather be a roper than a doper." He fell at the crux, stretching the rope so much he grazed a ledge at the bottom, but he got back on and struggled to the top, where he belly-flopped to safety, kicking the air. His effort prompted Reg to make a life-changing request. He wanted to lead.

He didn't care that the holds were hard to see, that the other party was competent or that leading took knowledge and practice. I didn't admit that I had chosen the climb partly to show off. Instead, I convinced myself that as long as he clipped the rope to at least one of the bolts, I could catch him when he fell. It would look cool when he gave up and I completed the climb for him. Also, according to playground morals, I wasn't really responsible for an older brother.

Reg clipped the rope to the higher bolt before clipping the lower one, so it tugged at his waist as he climbed. He didn't know that some of the face was easier and some of it was harder, so he just chinned past the hardest part without using his feet. He had no protection on the last 50 feet. Since I expected him to give up near the bottom, I hadn't given him any nuts or even told him what they were.

It was a relief when Reg reached the top, but Sig Isaac, a climber my age with a mop of black hair and South Asian features, nodded approvingly and told Reg he had done a nice lead. Sig's partner, Pete Reilly, who had a square jaw and the upper body of a linebacker, smiled when he added that Reg "almost bit it."

I had seen Sig and Pete working their way through harder climbs, but we had spoken little. They had a rope and carabiners but wore two-dollar canvas deck shoes with crepe soles. Some of their climbing methods were improvised, as mine had once been. Reg's wild lead should have stopped me from trying to be an authority on safety, but it didn't. I asked Sig if his anchor – not the usual bowline but a couple of half hitches – was safe.

"It won't come undone. What else matters?" he said.

"Finger size," said Pete. "Let me see your hand." He opened a broad palm from which five thick fingers protruded. I held my hand against his. My fingers were slightly thinner. He said he was on a finger diet.

Pete swigged from a plastic bottle of cola and started up Two Pieces, a committing little climb on a smooth face. He complained about how hard it was but showed no symptoms of fatigue or fear. After the climb, he said it had been easier than he had expected. At first I was confused, but after several more climbs with Pete, I figured out that you could only tell how hard a climb was for him by watching him climb and ignoring what he said while he did it. Taciturn British climbers I met years later in Yosemite said they'd been puzzled by a Canadian who bitched while he climbed but said everything had been easy afterwards. I wasn't surprised when they said his name was Pete.

Sig's friendship with Pete started on the high-school cross-country team in Don Mills, a suburb on the opposite side of the city from Etobicoke. They had bonded while training in a suffering-crazed era of running, when the city was home to athletes like Jerome Drayton who sacrificed everything to improve their race times. Perhaps it was running that gave Pete the idea of using a stopwatch to time his ascents.

Pete and Sig wanted to test themselves in less-controlled settings than running courses, but at first all they could afford was scrambling in the caves on the cliffs near Milton. While they were hiking at Rattlesnake, a climber let them tie into his rope and belayed them on an easy climb. Instantly smitten, they bought a yellow polypropylene rope and borrowed climbing books from the public library. After melting their plastic rope rappelling, they pooled their money for a real climbing rope and a few carabiners. Seasoned climbers who might show them a trick with a rope would also warn them to go slowly, so they taught themselves.

Life had taught Pete and Sig to move fast and be self-reliant. Sig had lived with his mother until partway through high school, when she moved to the Maritimes. He stayed behind in a tent in the Don River ravine because he didn't want to miss the spring running season. Hunger didn't prevent him from getting As and setting school records at meets.

Pete and his mother lived in a ranch-style bungalow near the four-lane highway of the Don Valley Parkway. She mainly spoke Hungarian, and Pete seemed to be her most important source of information about the world. His father lived somewhere in Toronto but didn't seem to have any more control over Pete than his mother did. Pete mainly did what he liked.

He nailed pieces of wood to the ceiling of the garage to create the first artificial climbing wall I had seen. Some of the problems were harder than those on the real climbs we tried. Special holds were designed to make his fingers leaner. He suspected thin fingers were my advantage, although he climbed better than me without them. Despite his ability, he took climbing less seriously than we did, because he was already planning what he would do afterwards. He yearned for adult responsibilities, while his climbing friends' indifference to anything but climbing was quickly increasing. He was the only one in our little group who wanted to have what was considered a normal life.

Our group was small. Apart from George Manson's circle, most climbers were graduates of top-roping courses. They had fun and seemed to avoid the perils of leading but were limited, since anything higher than half a rope couldn't be top-roped. We also felt there was something delusive about their obsession with safety, which could be evasive, even for top-ropers. The two Milton climbers killed in my early climbing years both fell from cliff edges while setting up top-ropes. Part of the problem was that guidebooks only described how climbs looked from the bottom of the cliff, where you started climbing. Top-ropers had to blindly find the top of climbs to set up. It was easy to imagine accidents happening after seeing the morning spectacle of top-ropers thrashing the bushes above the crag while shouting to the climbers waiting at the base, asking if they could see waving branches or bits of rope dangled over the edge. Usually they were nowhere close and took a long time to hang the rope in the right place. Competition to set up the ropes was often intense and there were arguments when two top-ropers found the correct place to drop their ropes at the same time. It was no wonder they left their ropes in place all day. To go through all that to avoid injury, you had to fear it more than average teenagers like us did.

Reg climbed as if he wanted to prove that teenage immortality wasn't just a delusion. He threw himself at climbs before he knew how protection worked. Sensible cragsmen warned him or refused to be close by when he climbed. By the spring of 1979, Rattlesnake Point, an outcrop of the same stone as McGillivray's Hill, was an arcadia that had in some ways replaced the lost farm. He had rock shoes instead of Davy Crockett moccasins, carabiners rather than a pellet gun, and instead of a groundhog's or rabbit's life, his own was at stake. He acted like it was a good trade.

I usually chose climbs based on books or on other climbers' advice. Reg just assumed he could do everything. His main love was free soloing, or climbing without a rope. Although free soloing was touted in *Mountain* as the purest way to climb, Reg hadn't read foreign climbing magazines. He had, however, grown up watching TV in the age of exhibitionist stuntmen.

When Evel Knievel, the king of stuntmen, tried to jump the Snake River Canyon on his rocket-powered motorcycle a few years earlier, he had crashed on the canyon floor. As soon as he could move his accelerator foot again, he jumped 14 buses. He claimed to have broken every bone in his body. He had only broken 35 out of 206, but it was still a world record. Knievel said that he had done his stunts to keep kids safe from drugs but he must have caused a global wave of broken bones among juvenile copycats.

We had aped Knievel, making jumps out of planks for our bikes in the summer and freezing sheets of plywood into the hillsides in the winter to jump in our plastic, super-slider, snow skates. When adults fretted about stitches and casts, we made the jumps higher. Reg rode his bike down a hill near our house and across the four-lane artery of Islington Avenue without braking. Neighbourhood troublemaker Ricky Schwarz claimed to have done it with his eyes closed. No one believed him until he did it blindfolded while we watched. Whether Knievel's evil lived on in Reg or he just had his own brand of fearlessness, he was often seen ropeless, a giant chalk bag hanging from his shorts, risking his life on routes only a grade or two easier than he could lead without falling off.

Reg preferred the East Cliff because its overhangs discouraged top-roping, and the unreliable rock favoured guts over precision. A few forbidding routes there still had an *A* next to them in the guidebook, because even George and his friends hadn't climbed them without rope ladders, hammers and pitons.

The wall had first been explored by Gerard Clement, a Frenchman working in Toronto in the '60s. He had trained outside Paris on the sandstone boulders of Fontainebleau, and in Ontario discovered the bouldering cliff known as Sunset Rock. He had also made the first ascents of the hardest climbs on the East Cliff, including the black overhanging wall he named the Spider.

My first nursery rhyme had been about a spider in a water spout. My father had told me how Scottish King Robert the Bruce regrouped his forces to fight the English after watching a spider's repeated attempts to climb a cave wall. Despite its relentlessness, the spider was more loathed than admired. Children feared its poisonous bite and its climbing ability. Spider-Man was a normal kid until a radioactive spider's sting gave him both the power and the impulse to climb buildings. Sometimes Pete used Spider-Man's catchphrase "Spidey-senses on" when he reached a tough section of rock. The spider was a symbol of whores, vampires, poisoners and predators, but climbers admired it. The Cassin Ridge on Denali, North America's highest peak, was first climbed by a team from northern Italy that called itself the Spiders. Heinrich Harrer's martyrology of the north face of the Eiger was named *The White Spider*. A cliff was the only place where being told you were behaving like a spider was a compliment.

Reg had only been climbing for a few months, but he had already led the Spider. On a midsummer afternoon, I watched him climb a few feet up it without a rope. I thought he was just bouldering and that he would climb down, but he didn't. Fifty feet higher, he reached an overhang where he began breathing heavily and a tremor in his heels showed he was struggling to keep his feet on the small holds. If he fell, he would die, and a fall seemed seconds away.

I rushed to the top of the cliff. Reg held on until I lowered him a rope. He attached it to his webbing chalk bag belt just as he popped off and swung into space. I lowered him to the talus. When I got back down, his eyes were iridescent with fear. He said he could have made it, but I didn't believe it. Maybe he didn't either, but saying so kept our world habitable. We panted in the building heat, breathing the fragrances of the woods and warm stone. In that moment, just being alive felt like a stunt.

Others who kicked away the ladder of rope and gear relied more on knowledge than guts. Dave Lanman and Pete Reilly soloed almost at the level they led, although unlike Reg they tended to choose routes they knew well. Mostly they were just indulging the urge to try going without a rope on climbs that they had already done dozens of times without incident. Eventually they soloed all but the hardest climbs, and as they did so, they drifted into a world that normalized the possibility of dying for a rock climb.

Ironically, instead of making me bolder, my handful of hard unroped climbs made me wonder whether I was brave enough to be a climber at all. Soloing, I might prance upwards, exhilarated by the brilliant rock and my own technique. It was just as likely, however, that something as trivial as the sight of my shadow on the talus could make me realize how vulnerable I was. The soloist who has lost his nerve is like a prisoner digging his own grave, whose every action hastens the bullet. The tension between the two moods was addictive, but eventually everyone had to kick the habit. After one of Reg's wild public solos, George Manson told him he would die if he used similarly poor judgement on El Capitan. Since I was standing close by, he added that the same went for me. He didn't realize it, but my ropeless days were all but over. The curse strengthened my secret fear of big-wall climbing, which fed my sense that it was precisely a big wall that would test my worth.

Reg grumbled that George was so far beyond us that his advice didn't apply, especially since he was passing into yet another, even more advanced realm of climbing. That summer George would attempt the Cassin Ridge. By then, some top Yosemite climbers had torn up the icefalls and alpine faces of the Canadian Rockies, the Alps and Alaska. Rock climbing in Yosemite was so far ahead of everywhere else that Valley masters' alpine forays were seen almost as inevitable victory marches. Fast ascents of hard Rockies routes, the first ascent of the Dru Couloir Direct in the Mont Blanc massif, a solo of the hardest route on the north face of the Eiger and many other successes made it seem like falling rock, avalanches and extreme cold didn't make much difference if you could climb 5.12.

If that's what it took, could Manson's team, with its own Yosemite credentials also succeed? I had no idea. Books offered a glimpse into the world of the alpine climber. Glacier travel, reading snow conditions, rock climbing in crampons and countless other mountain skills were such dark arts to me that on my first alpine climbs I would tiptoe as quickly as

I could across glaciers to the rock walls in my sneakers, as if treading lightly might protect me from being swallowed by a crevasse. That was on a rock peak in a small range of which real alpinists took little account. The Cassin's nine thousand feet of glaciers, ice and snow-covered rock led to the highest summit in North America. In night photographs the mountain blotted out the stars, suggesting cold and dangers beyond the limits of my dreams and reasoning.

CHAPTER 6

The Thieves' Den

I can't remember when I first did a famous hard Gunks route, but I can remember many of those climbs handhold by handhold. In fact, I knew a lot about the handholds before I even tried these climbs. Erect Directions, for example, had a traverse under a roof that ended when I ran out of wall and had to hook my heel over my head and pull myself over the overhang. The crux on Erect Directions was a couple of hundred feet up, with lots of open air below, but I was relieved of having to figure out this unlikely move; I knew how to do it because I had seen it in a magazine photo. Many of the climbs I did in the Gunks were well recorded in photos, print or stories handed down from climber to climber. The routes weren't just incidents of geology, they were monuments to the climbing history of the area.

Most Ontario climbers at the time either top-roped for

fun or practiced for the Rockies by leading easy climbs. They cared little about the history of their own area or the world of serious rock climbing of which the Gunks was a part. The Gunks was my first chance to dip my toe in the mainstream of climbing history and tradition.

Toronto was a huge and growing city, so there were always a few good climbers who ended up there, despite the fact the climbing was not renowned. The climbing in the Gunks, however, was good enough to attract some of the world's best climbers. Steve Wunsch came from Colorado to climb Supercrack at Skytop, one of the hardest climbs America. Yosemite's Ron Kauk made the second ascent. New England's "Hot" Henry Barber, in an Andy Capp slouch-hat he picked up showing off his skills on British outcrops, added dozens of tough routes.

In the Gunks, even the climbing store was classier. A lot of Toronto climbers bought their gear in an army surplus outlet on a section of Yonge Street populated by drug dealers and hookers. The climbing supplier in the Gunks was world famous and advertised in *Mountain*. Local specialists like John Bragg and Kevin Bein could be spotted in the climbing store buying nuts on wire as thin as guitar strings to replace those they had snapped falling off improbably blank walls. There were photos of the cliffs of the Shawangunk Mountains in Chris Jones's history of climbing, and Jim Mark's guide had a note about them.

In the Adirondacks, when Tad and Fred killed rain time describing the Gunks and Judy got stoned, I was intrigued. But I could not have predicted the role the Gunks would play in my life.

The Gunks is a three-hundred-foot-high quartzite conglomerate escarpment in the Catskills, just north of New York City. In the 1930s, immigrants from alpine Europe and patrician Americans who holidayed in the Alps started climbing there. There were clapboard Jewish resort hotels instead of chalets, and the rocks were a tenth of the height of big mountain crags, but the cliffs were only an hour or two away from millions of people on the eastern seaboard, and the climbs proved engaging and difficult. They were also in range of Montreal and Toronto, and some Canadian climbers had new route credits in the guidebooks.

The Gunks rose from a landscape disarmingly similar to the countryside I was used to, with its ancient farms, disused fencelines and fast, narrow creeks. The climbers were city-based, like us. On weekends, their cars lined the roads below the cliffs, and the best routes were climbed many times.

Climbers accessed the Trapps, the highest and most popular cliff, by a carriage road that passed jumbled outcrops known as the Uberfall. There we scrambled down after higher climbs farther along the face. The climbers in head scarves, bouldering, drinking from the artesian well or looking for rope partners, made the Uberfall look like the thieves' den local legend said it once was.

At the Uberfall, a ranger sold dollar tickets for a day's climbing from the back of his pickup truck. The money must have been barely enough to pay him, let alone support the upkeep costs and liability insurance of the Smiley family, who owned most of the cliffs. The fee could be reduced even further by buying a $15 button for a whole season's climbing, yet many climbers believed that climbing should be free, so they kept their dollar and snuck up to the cliffs through the talus.

Visiting climbers could stay for free in a mouldy farmhouse that a gunshot-perforated sign declared to be the property of the Appalachian Mountain Club. In the '60s, the Appies, as the members of the club were known, reacted to a fatal climbing accident by trying to impose a certification system on climbers. The Vulgarians, hard climbers from New York City, drank heavily, climbed nude and dismissed certification as prudery.

The Appies and the Vulgarians were gone by the time I started climbing in the Gunks, but by the appearance of the house on most weekend nights, the Vulgarians had won. Climbers from across the East Coast sat talking about road trips or the day's adventures, rolling joints, swilling bad red wine and draining beer cans. It was common to be woken by noisy lovers.

I went to the Gunks many times with many different

people, but usually I was with Dave Lanman, Reg, Pete Reilly, Sig Isaac or Judy Paddon. The rituals of the trip included driving there as fast as possible without getting ticketed and boasting about what we would climb. Sometimes, we were so eager that we left Toronto after work or school and arrived in the early hours of the morning.

On my first trip to the Gunks with Judy, in October 1978, we carpooled with Alan and Greg, undergraduates young enough to find top-roping a little dull, but old enough to seem like adults to us. Al was an unflappable belayer, and Greg was an aggressive leader who had the unusual habit of casually falling off when leading. Judy and I sat quietly in the back seat as Greg played tapes of ska bands he had mail-ordered from England, and explained them to a skeptical Alan, who preferred gossiping about college parties. Judy didn't want to talk about climbing or ska and spent the drive knitting.

We arrived at the hut in the early evening on a Monday. All that remained of the weekend crowds were a few empty bottles and Dave. He had hung some old sheets from the low rafters of the second floor to make a little room, where he put his sleeping bag and climbing gear.

I introduced Dave and he smiled broadly, solicited Al and Greg's climbing level and recommended a torrent of climbing routes, all accompanied with gestures imitating the cruxes. He then explained with aristocratic unconcern that he was broke and stranded. Charmed, they agreed to drive him to

New Paltz in the morning to pick up his girlfriend, who was coming by bus from Montreal and was bringing money. Dave said she would busk on the street as a mime and make them some money.

The next morning, Dave squeezed into the back seat with Judy and me for the drive to town. She asked what he knew about the college in New Paltz.

"Nothing, but check it out." He put a hand on her knee, leaned across her lap and pointed. "That cliff with a castle's Skytop. That overhang is Foops. I did it last week." He seemed to expect her to squeal in delight, but she didn't. "It's 5.11," he said, and sunk back into his seat.

Judy didn't look at the overhang but put down her knitting needles and asked if I wanted to.

The town had an old college that was now the state university and a cemetery dating back to the French Huguenots, who had settled there in the 17th century. The Dutch had followed and named the streams and rocks: Peterskill, Wallkill, Trapps.

There were echoes of the 1960s. Vegetarian restaurants and a head shop thrived on the three-block Main Street strip. A white-haired man dressed like a gypsy swept the streets. He was said to have settled in town after a bad trip at the Woodstock Festival, which was held in nearby Bethel in 1969.

At the climbing store that day, I met Hugh Herr, a high-school freshman and a top Gunks climber. When he was eight years old, he had climbed to the 11,000-foot summit of Mount Temple with his father. He had also made the first ascents of difficult alpine rock routes in the Bugaboos and ticked off many of the hardest Gunks climbs. His Mennonite parents were from Pennsylvania, and he commuted to the Gunks on weekends with his brother, Tony, who was also a good climber. Two years later, I climbed with Hugh for a couple of days in Yosemite. He was as gifted but more driven and prolific than Dave, whose climbing competed with a bohemian streak.

Back home, Dave Lanman still had no real equals in climbing. In the bars of New Paltz, however, top climbers from Europe and the western states were resting up to try hard climbs like Supercrack, Gravity's Rainbow or Kansas City. Climbing was even the theme of bathroom graffiti. I saw a man scrawl an insult about a 5.12 on the wall above a urinal. The only place climbers avoided was a bar with neon Budweiser signs that filled on weekend nights with tough-looking cadets from West Point.

Despite its stature in the climbing world, New Paltz was so small that the only way to get there by public transportation was the bus. We joined a few greeters on the New York Trailways platform to wait for Dave's girlfriend. The bus arrived, but after the passengers had shuffled down the stairs to their loved ones and the driver had shut the luggage compartments, there was no girlfriend.

"You waiting for a girl from Canada?" the driver asked. "Hippie girl?"

Dave asked if she was asleep in her seat. The driver laughed grimly. The driver had left her in a hospital emergency ward upstate. Dave gawped. The driver said Dave could call the hospital or wait to see if she came on another bus. Dave went to find a pay phone. Judy wanted to stay with him, but I wanted her to belay, and there was nothing she could do to help Dave anyway. We left him in town and went climbing.

We were both soon distracted. The easy routes of the Gunks were more fun than similarly graded climbs anywhere else. We wound across faces seamed with horizontal ledges like giant ladder rungs and swung like monkeys from cracks in overhangs. We took on white open faces with thin cracks just wide enough for a finger or a wired nut. Even on easy routes, the faces peppered with quartzite crystals and small edges had complicated crux moves that would be tricky to climb down.

Our fingers were raw and our arms were tired when we returned to the old farmhouse at twilight. As we made sandwiches for dinner, the wind brought the smell of moss and dead chestnut leaves through the bare window frames.

Dave and his girlfriend were upstairs. She smiled, but her dark eyelids made her seem a little sad. Her hair was tangled and she wore a ragged Jimi Hendrix T-shirt. She looked older than Dave, but she wasn't. Greg tried to get her to talk about music, assuming that anyone who climbed would be cool enough to be up-to-date on his favourite subject, but she frustrated him by nodding and saying she didn't know anything about punk rock. She said she was part of the Hendrix generation, pointing to her shirt.

At the top of the wooden staircase, Dave tried to boil water on a brass camp stove. It spurted flaming gas, threatening to trap us if the floor caught fire. Greg opened his mouth, but before he could speak, Dave told him to relax.

"I'm sleeping downstairs," said Greg, "near the door."

Judy and I spoke a little to Dave's girlfriend. She seemed to have recovered completely from taking what she described as a "funky cap and stem." Those could be cool, Dave said. He'd even taken one on El Capitan, and it had been fine. Months later I figured out that they were talking about hallucinogenic mushrooms.

She told us that Brandy Greenwood, the boy whom I had met at SEE whose father was a famous climber, had introduced her to Dave. She had dropped out of SEE to climb with him and be a mime. Her teacher had studied with Marcel Marceau, who I only knew because he was spoofed in a Monty Python skit.

Al, Greg, Judy and I slept downstairs until a noise of creaking and snapping boards woke us. Greg said someone should splash water on the couple upstairs. We woke up late to see Sig and Reg, who had driven all night from Toronto, sitting in the corner. I told them about the noise, and they looked upstairs, but Dave and his girlfriend had left for the cliff. Sig stepped on a board and it squeaked a little. Reg jumped up and down, adding a faint creak, nothing like the racket from the night before.

Judy said she liked New Paltz and wanted to spend the day exploring the university, cafés and alternative bookstore. Sig and Reg hiked to Skytop, and Greg and Alan were off for their first day on the faces of the Trapps. Partnerless, I bouldered at the Uberfall with Dave as his girlfriend sat cross-legged and read. He wanted to climb at Near Trapps, a cliff across the road from the Uberfall that bristled with overhangs.

After pulling on tattered rock shoes and tying into the rope, Dave started up like a boxer coming out of his corner. It was one thing to see him on his home crags, where he knew every climb, but here all he had to rely on was his talent. It was a revelation. Even on rocks he had not climbed before, his footwork was as precise as a dancer's and his hands grasped the holds as confidently as a workman brandishing his tools. He seemed unable to panic. Above an overhang he slid tiny wired nuts into shallow cracks and clipped them to the rope with a piece of greying tubular webbing.

Dave didn't wait to see if I would follow his example; he cajoled me into being a better climber. If I just looked at an overhang, he'd start convincing me to try it. He would say it was easy, use terms of endearment like *dude*, act like we both climbed at the same level, say it was over-graded, whether or not it was, and pantomime the movement to make it look as simple as climbing a ladder. It often worked. He was the lens through which I experienced my first hard Gunks climbs. He helped me to overcome my limitations and corrupted me with the ambition of becoming some kind of cool expert. Where inspiration ended and ambition began never mattered.

On our last day I was on my own at the Uberfall.

Judy had gone into town to call her parents. Dave and his girlfriend were climbing an easy route I had already done. Alan and Greg were cramming in a final route. Reg and Sig were climbing too, discovering the partnership that would serve them in the years to come. I tried to find a partner at the Uberfall, but although I belayed Hugh Herr on an over-hang I couldn't second, I didn't climb. I didn't care. I was in the Gunks.

My feeling for the place grew as I did. There, I achieved several climbing goals that were the main currency of success in the youth I had chosen, ordered my first drink, stayed in tents, ditches, huts and cheap hotels. I was there in snow, rain, fog and the crushing heat of summer. I climbed there with men who quit climbing and became soft or went on to other, harder things, and with some who died young in their sports cars, were crushed by icicles or disappeared on Himalayan peaks. I climbed with a few whose names will be remembered in the history of climbing and with those who never climbed again after their first day. I found things there I wasn't looking for and carelessly threw away things I would one day miss.

Driving home, Greg and Alan played tapes and argued about who was seen as a more outrageous drunk at college. Judy showed me a book about vegetarianism she had bought in New Paltz. She said she would never eat meat again. Wool, however, was all right because it was inedible and didn't require killing animals. I saw knitting as her excuse to withdraw from everyone, including me. As the hours ticked by, I tried to think of a devastating argument against vegetarianism. It was no use; my mind kept drifting to my next climbing day.

A month later, my father went to Mexico City on a lecture trip. My mother couldn't go, so he invited me to come with him. After I spent a few days wandering around the city on my own, a friend of one of his students took me up a dormant volcano. Although the top was almost 18,000 feet above sea level, the slope was gradual enough to have first been climbed by conquistadors gathering sulphur for gunpowder. Looking out over the dark brown haze of Mexico City, I was breathless and poisoned by bad water, and my climbing partner spoke no English, but I wasn't cold. I was wearing the sweater I had watched Judy manically knitting on the way home from the Gunks. She had wanted to finish it in time for my trip.

CHAPTER 7

Sophocles

In September of 1978, after my year of ignoring schoolwork at SEE, my parents made me return to a regular school. My mother once again wanted me to go to upper-middle-class Richview, but I ended up back at Etobicoke Collegiate. I felt like a convict returned to his prison after being on the lam.

Training and reading offered some relief from the monotony of my weekdays. Having read all of the climbing books I could, I discovered other writers, some of whom I found in crumbling paperback anthologies my father had bought in his romantic undergraduate days. Decadent poetry inspired me to see the little rebellion I was living out in the forests and crags at the suburbs' edge as part of youth's eternal longing for more.

This romanticism reflected and heightened my sense of isolation. After William stopped climbing, we hardly talked to each other. Since there was no one to discuss climbing with at my school, I hardly spoke to anyone. Sig Isaac and Pete Reilly lived on the opposite side of town, and I only saw them when I climbed. Reg had a full-time job. My marks disappointed my father. My mother fretted about having climbing sons. Perhaps we reminded her of the men of her family who had become unemployed cads after their adventurous youths, or my cousin and his useless preoccupation with science fiction. It was, however, a relief that my parents focused their efforts on my sisters, who had good marks and no dangerous hobbies.

Climbing compromised school but enabled me to graduate to Yosemite Valley, the place I had read about and gawked at in books and magazines for years. Dave Lanman had climbed the Shield on El Capitan. George Manson, Mike Tschipper and Tom Gibson all spoke about Yosemite as if it was their home. The new photo book *Yosemite Climber*, edited by California guidebook writer George Meyers, was a window to paradise. Its photos showed climbers in ragged clothes flexing Olympic physiques on fiendish rock climbs. Between climbs they sunbathed, drank beer, smoked marijuana and lifted weights in the climbers' hangout known as Camp Four.

Although Yosemite's walls were vastly bigger than Milton's, there were climbers who used the local cliffs to stay fit for Yosemite. On the weekends I tried doing 20 or 30 routes in a day, dreaming that I was simulating a long climb in Yosemite. In fact, most Yosemite pitches were twice as long as the average pitch at Rattlesnake and the style of climbing was quite different, but my options were limited.

Getting to the Valley would have been a challenge if Dave Moore and Brian Hibbert hadn't invited me to come with them in exchange for helping out with their courses. Mistakes like setting up the wrong climbs or free soloing in front of the students were met by my bosses' old-school barracking. It wasn't politically correct, but it was more useful than the advice I was getting from most adults.

If anything, watching me prepare for my big trip made my usual partners climb more than I did. Reg's skill with equipment had grown with his strength. Sig and Pete seemed stronger every time I saw them. The grace and commitment of Sig's climbing made his rare errors more dramatic. On a crack that should have been easy for him, he slotted his fingers on top of a nut without realizing it. The nut came loose and he fell. His feet grazed the ground as the rope went taut.

Pete Reilly's enthusiastic coaching, which included using a stopwatch, was powered by the cola he drank to suppress his appetite. His main worry was that he would put fat on his thick fingers, making it harder to grasp small holds. While he was climbing, his bitching made difficult moves sound harder, but his great technique made the same moves look easy.

It had always been hard to imagine Dave Lanman in school, and now he gave it up to drift between the Gunks, where he began to cultivate a reputation as a hard climber; Montreal, where his girlfriend lived; and Toronto, where he had family and work. He earned a pittance dishwashing or guarding crosswalks but embodied the philosophy of Italian climber Walter Bonatti, who saw nobility in any job that allowed him to climb.

We saw little of George Manson, Tom Gibson and Mike Tschipper that winter. George, Sean Lewis – who had climbed the Lotus Flower Tower with George – a man from the Alpine Club named Dave Carroll whom I had never met, and Alan Chase, an alpinist from Maine, were headed for the Cassin Ridge. In the spring they travelled west to ready themselves for what was still one of the most feared climbs on the continent.

Dave Moore and Brian Hibbert shortened their après-climbing bar sessions to practice Yosemite tactics like aid climbing, using pitons and crawling up ropes with mechanical ascenders called jumars. I had no talent for complicated rope techniques and just climbed, hoping to figure out what I needed to do when I needed to do it. Brian and Dave needed to be more deliberate. Climbing stole time from the families and careers that also restrained them from taking risks. My friends and I had little sympathy for these adult burdens.

It wasn't coincidental that Gerry Banning, the only adult to join our group, had few apparent grown-up responsibilities. You didn't have to try to meet Gerry. Comb-over bandana'd in place, he strode the talus, hailing climbers or belting out opera arias that seemed all the louder for his squat muscleman physique. He had grown up in a northern mining town where he had attended a one-room schoolhouse. Hungry for experience, he took climbing courses, sung in an opera chorus and paid ten bucks for *pommes frites* in fancy restaurants. He bought shirts and pants from Italian tailors who measured him after the shop was closed. The clothes soon bored him and he gave them to us. A double layer of Italian gabardine was warm enough for ice climbing.

Gerry lived in a commune in a rambling Victorian house in a once-gritty neighbourhood in the east end of Toronto that was later the setting of Michael Ondaatje's *In the Skin of a Lion*. The reek of marijuana, shelves of empty wine bottles and dusty piles of books on Maoism and women's rights gave it a decaying charm. Gerry's room, however, was spotless and decorated with austere modern furniture and a poster from the 1954 musical *The Student Prince*.

The first meal Gerry and I shared was at a Greek seafood restaurant with a ten-foot-high concrete statue of a naked man. Gerry talked about his life as he ate octopus-ink spaghetti and invited me to work out with him at the YMCA. I went, and although the disco aerobics felt ridiculous, he showed me some useful tricks with the dumbbells.

Gerry read the latest books about how to be happy or master personal weaknesses. "It's just Chinese food for the mind," he said, urging me to read them too, but I never did. One of his favourite subjects was how the 1960s had shown him that suffering was square and being OK was what it was all about. This philosophy caused his climbing to stall out before his teenage friends' did – for them, fear and suffering were antidotes to boredom. It was a dilemma. Were they as crazy as other people who weren't OK and didn't know what it was all about? If he wanted to climb harder would he have to become not OK too?

A sport psychology paperback offered a solution: staving off panic by reciting the name of an animal. Gerry chose the tiger. He first unleashed his power animal on a steep climb on the East Cliff. It was the ominously named Crack-Up. Reg, who had climbed the route, belayed and gave advice.

Around the corner, Dave Lanman and I were trying an unclimbed overhang. We tried laybacking it, cramming our fingertips into it and even leaping past it to a ledge. After many falls, we sat at the base, discussing what to try next, when we heard Gerry's baritone voice booming out the name of his power animal. There was a thud and clatter as he fell. His cry weakened to a plea, and there was silence.

Although the psychology books were as useless to me as they were to Gerry, I am indebted to him for the gift of a couple of how-to books about writing and editing. At school I had memorized grammar and spelling by rote. Gerry's books said that grammar and spelling weren't goals in themselves, but tools I could use to express myself. Although my father had written a shelf full of scientific books and articles, I assumed they were full of inscrutable research (which they only partly were) and never suspected that I had inherited the desire to write. Whether Gerry's books awakened innate abilities or just inspired the conceit that I could be a writer, they sowed the seeds of a harvest of articles, a handful of climbing guidebooks and, eventually, a career in editing.

Reg and Gerry made their first climbing trip with Judy and me in early summer, 1979. We went to the oldest rock climbing area in eastern Canada, Val-David, north of Montreal, where the vertical granite cracks were a little like Yosemite's. Gerry, Judy and I piled into Reg's Hornet, and he drove all the way to Val-David because Gerry and I didn't have licences and Reg didn't trust Judy Paddon at the wheel.

In Montreal we bought poutine from a café with a *hot dog frites* sign. A crude pictograph of the FLQ habitant with pipe and gun decorated the wall of a shop next door. Nearby, a store that sold old-fashioned belay claws and ring pitons also had a climbing guidebook for the Laurentians. A tourist map said Val-David was an hour from Montreal and named after a president of the Montreal Canadiens who had been received into the *Légion d'honneur*.

We set up our nylon pup tents at a road head near Mont Condor, just outside of the village. Judy told me her plans. Science had been her strength but not SEE's. At a regular school, she could study hard and finish quickly. She wanted to go to McGill University in Montreal, which was good for science and closer to the Gunks than Toronto. I was silent. I had only been in Montreal for about an hour and didn't know how I felt about it. She said I had helped her make the decision, although we had never discussed it. I think it was meant as a compliment, but I was still confused when I went to sleep after hours of staring at the tent wall.

At first light, Gerry shook our tents, asking if we wanted to jog. We didn't. He returned to find us scooping cereal out of a box with our hands. Reg offered him some. After driving to a store where he bought paper plates and plastic spoons, Gerry ate breakfast in the parking lot and explained that because he needed a shower, we should commute to the cliff from his brother's house in Montreal. I was ambivalent. It seemed ironic that Reg would sleep on the floor of a suburban rec room on his first climbing trip, but we packed our camping gear and commuted both ways from Gerry's brother's house in the suburbs.

Val-David's cliffs were as busy as Rattlesnake Point. The climbers had a mixture of old-fashioned Rébuffat rope ladders with aluminum rungs and the white pants and headbands that were popular in the US. There were more pitons in the cliffs than there were in Ontario; a three-hundred-foot climb at nearby Weir had one every three feet. Despite the Old World touches, the best climbers in Quebec were ahead of most Ontario climbers, with ascents of huge cliffs in eastern Quebec and some long ice routes almost as challenging as any in North America at the time.

Although eastern Quebec had some very high cliffs, Val-David's crags were about the same height as those of Milton. I had only been on granite cracks once, in the Adirondacks, and I wanted to try my first, hard, finger-width fissure. Most of the hardest rock climbs of the world were finger cracks back then, and they were common in Yosemite, although not on the limestone faces I was used to. Near the top of my first finger crack, I ran out of strength and fell. Judy locked the rope in the belay plate just before I hit the talus. It was my first long leader fall, and the combination of fear and adrenaline was nauseating. I had fallen almost 40 feet, although I had only been a few feet above my last piece of protection and should have gone half that distance.

Reg was standing close by and said that Judy hadn't been paying attention because she was feeding my lunch to a squirrel. I said nothing, but after overhearing Reg's accusation, Judy said she would stay in Montreal the next day instead of climbing.

At Mont King the next morning, I found a belayer for a vertical face more like the climbs I had done at home. My annoyance with being left on my own, and the knowledge that it might be the only climb I got to do that day, made me climb with resolve. A girl with blue eyes and black hair climbing nearby said she had seen me the day before. She made a flying motion with her hand. My girlfriend hadn't been watching, I said, but she likes squirrels. When she climbed she wiggled her hips and made a clumsy joke about the route name. Afterwards, she thanked me, untied and walked away down the cliff.

Much later, I met her at Rattlesnake, and she remembered my name. We watched a movie about a young violinist struggling to master a quartet by Ravel. She cried a little at the end.

She told me about her years in the Alps as the mistress of a rich Austrian. Her story was full of betrayals, helicopters and raw emotions. Listening to it drained me. Then she said it was just a story, that she was full of shit. She asked me why I didn't like her when we first met.

"I was thinking about climbing. It was all I was thinking about."

"But you had a girlfriend – the English girl?"

"I did, but I was only thinking about climbing."

She said she didn't believe it. There was something else. I was bullshitting, she said, like her.

Dave Lanman's brother Steve told me about a job at the private summer school where he was a bus driver. It was a 90-minute subway and bus trip away, but work was scarce and I planned to quit and go to Yosemite halfway through the summer anyway. For $100 a week, I washed dishes in a damp, hot shed. It wasn't the worst job I would do to climb, it was just the worst job I had done so far. In the coming years I would dig ditches and carry lead pipes in 40-below temperatures, wash dishes in a dozen restaurants, rivet together appliances on an assembly line and staple lining into coffins.

At the camp, I mostly worked with long-haired, pimply heavy-metal fans who pedalled rusty ten-speeds to work. Their prize possessions were fake ID cards they used to buy the beer they drank in local ravines.

I had grown up with guys like these, but the better-paid counsellors were mainly kids from the school's neighbourhood, which was one of the wealthiest in the country. I only got to know one of them. Angela had long, delicate fingers, freckles, brown eyes, fine manners and a spiky punk haircut.

One night after work, I walked towards the subway with her instead of taking the bus. We stopped at a park bench to talk. Although she discussed rock music with an almost academic rigour that might have been learned from her English-professor parents, she was becoming a little enemy of the adult world. A schoolmate had run away with her boyfriend. The schoolmate's parents were mad at Angela because she wouldn't reveal the girl's whereabouts. Her professed devotion to alcohol and drugs seemed noble in its disdain for possible consequences.

We walked in the dark past blocks of tall, stone-dressed facades and the shadows of topiary to a villa of white stucco and black, sloping gables. She invited me to a party the next week, said goodnight and stepped through a limestone arch into the yellow-lit vestibule. The subway had shut down and I walked home through canyons of apartment buildings to Etobicoke, arriving just before dawn.

Next Friday night, Reg and I stood in Angela's high-ceilinged, wood-panelled dining room in our checked flannel workmen's jackets. We drank beer from a case we had brought and watched kids with hairspray quiffs, sunglasses and blazers with thin lapels looting a well-stocked liquor cabinet. Angela wore a tight dress and leaned against the wall, sipping gin and brandishing a tiny hash pipe. She and a boy were locked in an intense conversation about music.

I looked for her later. I found her embracing the same boy on the bathroom floor. By now the partiers had exhausted the household alcohol supply and started eyeing our remaining beer. Reg and I went out to the front lawn and sat on a stone step. As we finished our last beers, a middle-aged man in a corduroy jacket and a paisley shirt ran up the stairs and through the open door. I assumed it was Angela's father returning to find her and her friend in the bathroom.

I told no one at work I was quitting, not even Angela. I just didn't show up the next day. The lost pay didn't matter. In a week I would be in Yosemite.

The next morning, I packed to climb. The thought that I wouldn't see Angela again concerned me less than the climb I was anticipating that day. The rickety, toy-like device I was stuffing in my pack filled me with a level of anticipation that hash pipes and gin bottles could not. It was a spring-loaded camming nut known as a Friend, and I had bought it to use on my last climb before going to Yosemite. British-built Friends were designed by aerospace engineer and Yosemite climbing ace Ray Jardine for parallel-sided and flaring cracks that wouldn't hold nuts. Terry Monk, a commercial pilot based in Oakville, near Toronto, imported them to North America and sold them out of his basement along with three-dollar Italian carabiners and inexpensive French climbing ropes. His gear was so cheap that you could buy it at retail, resell it in the US and still make a good profit. Even at 25 bucks, Friends cost almost ten times as much as nuts, but they were worth it. Placing a nut in a parallel-sided crack required the touch of a watchmaker, and, as I had learned in Val-David, it was harder with sweaty hands and forearms blocked with lactic acid. Placing a Friend in a similar crack was so simple that some climbers said they were cheating.

At noon the next day, sun blasted the walls of Rattlesnake. The air was dense with the tang of wild vines and the chalky smell of the rock. Reg and I dropped our packs below the leaning wall of the East Cliff. Uncoiling the rope, Reg discovered the opal-eyed corpse of a deer on a bed of ivy glistening with blood. One of its antlers had been struck off. Reg guessed coyotes had chased it off the cliff in the night. It was fresh enough to cut up for meat, he said, but he didn't have the right knife with him. The coyotes hadn't eaten it, he said, because they sometimes killed for practice, even if they weren't hungry.

I knew about it. I had seen a mouse scurry across wind-hardened snow at McGillivray's Hill as a fox loped along beside it, in no hurry to take its prey. I had shot groundhogs for kicks. Reg said it was like the poem I had told him about from the club meeting, but it wasn't. If I'd read more than a few lines of the poem at the Toronto Section meeting, I might have taken the carcass as a warning. It foreshadowed the hero's request to be pushed off the mountain after being paralyzed by a fall.

Reg changed the subject with a joke about how Angela had looked at the party and how stupid I was to have gone to it, since she obviously didn't think I was very cool. He said I should have spent the time getting ready for Yosemite, as if skipping a workout to see a girl defied some tenet of our religion. Anyway, he said, she was too good-looking for me.

Sophocles was one of the few climbs at Rattlesnake I hadn't done. It was an old aid route up a steep wall decorated with a couple of corroded and deformed pitons. The crux was an overhang 30 feet up, where a small black slot offered the first protection. After it had been free climbed by George, it retained a reputation for danger that prevented anyone I knew from trying it, even though it was a grade easier than the hardest climbs. I had no idea why the route was named after the Greek playwright, or even that he was a playwright.

If I had known that he once said, "The young people of to-day think of nothing but themselves. They have no rever-ence for parents or old age. They are impatient of all restraint. They talk as if they alone knew everything and what passes for wisdom with us is foolishness with them," I would have agreed with him, at least as far as climbing was concerned.

I climbed big, hot holds that forced me to lean out from the rock. A quick look at the sharp talus blocks below helped me focus on pulling back the triggers on the Friend and stick-ing it in the damp black crack. The crux was a mantelshelf, a move similar to getting out of a swimming pool, but with a leaning wall six inches from the pool's edge.

I stood slowly, hands correcting my balance on either side. The rock next to my face filled my nostrils with the smell of chalk, and I fought against falling backwards. My arms were stretched out so far I must have appeared crucified. The strug-gle between gravity and balance ended as I threw a hand to a big hold. I put a nut in a crack, clipped the rope to a carabi-ner and climbed to a belay ledge where stone walls formed a small, pale room.

CHAPTER 8

The Curse

At midday in August 1979, temperatures in Yosemite Valley hovered at 90 degrees Fahrenheit. The Valley's best climbers preferred the cooler temperatures of spring and fall, but Brian Hibbert and Dave Moore had to be back before the school year began. They had a list of routes that were in the shade, a pile of equipment and the latest guidebook. On the three-day drive, they sat in the front of Brian's station wagon, tuning in to country and western stations, jibing about spouses and jobs and discussing women with a mixture of expletive and innuendo. I sat in the back, trying to make sense of the Indian poems in the book Bea gave me, or staring at the photos in *Yosemite Climber*.

In my pocket was a temporary driver's permit known as a 365. I got it by taking a half-hour test to prove I could recognize basic road signs and markings. With a licensed driver present, I was allowed to drive wherever I wanted for a year. Or, at least, that's what I did. David and Brian were my driving instructors. The course was Interstate Highway 80, a transcontinental pinball playfield with potholes, 18-wheelers, Winnebagos and drag racers as kickers.

Brian twice grabbed the steering wheel to avoid a collision, but he let me drive. My steering improved with practice, and I barrelled across the High Plains until a Wyoming state trooper clocked me at 80 miles an hour. He pulled me over at dawn, below a billboard with the scowling face of the Ayatollah Khomeini and the caption "Fight back, drive 55." The national speed limit was meant to reduce accidents, but westerners separated by long, lonely highways loathed it like gun control, so it was repackaged as aggressive foreign policy. The trooper told me to pull into the next town and pay the fine at a courthouse, but Brian and David were asleep and I decided to ignore him. We were only an hour from the Utah border, and in cop shows, highway patrols couldn't cross state lines.

On the morning of the third day, we entered California and wound our way through the Sierra Mountains. The thousand-foot-high granite domes of Tuolumne Meadows rose beside the road. They seemed like the highest, smoothest, most beautiful rocks in the world, but they were soon put in perspective. After we passed through the tunnel along the base of Reed's Pinnacle, we beheld the walls of El Capitan, Sentinel and Cathedral rocks and, in the distance, the vertical hoop of

Half Dome. We tumbled out of the car onto the valley floor, where a river flowed through open meadows and deer cavorted as if we were in a live-action version of *Bambi*. We could barely make out the dots of climbers on giant El Capitan.

We soon learned more mundane truths about the Valley. Its wonders were protected by the rangers of the US National Park Service, who I only knew from Yogi Bear cartoons and Disney movies. Yosemite was as much the rangers' police state as a bucolic retreat. There was a murder during our stay, illegal Valley residents slept in the bathrooms and I was offered drugs within a couple hours of arriving. There were restaurants, laundromats, swimming pools and hotels, and we bought our food at a supermarket with a parking lot where a tow truck was busy removing illegally parked cars.

Campsites could only be reserved for a week at a time. After three consecutive weeks, campers had to leave Yosemite completely, as if their visas had expired. There was an hour-long lineup at a kiosk to collect the permit for a pre-booked site. A bulletin board's notes scribbled in a dozen languages asked for climbing partners, rides all over the continent and buyers for used gear.

We set up our tents on sun-scorched gravel just beyond the shade of the boulders and pines. On our first night we drank beer with our neighbours, a climbing club from a Japanese factory. Late in the evening, the leader said he could tell that Brian was a lady's man and showed him what appeared to be a Japanese pornographic magazine. Brian hummed, nodded and suppressed a smirk. When the beer ran out, the evening ended with handshakes and embraces. Brian laughed when I asked him about the magazine. All of the women had been fully clothed.

Brian and David chose Royal Arches as a first Yosemite climb because, although it was 1,500 feet long, it had no difficult pitches. The most exciting part was shimmying across a dead tree to avoid a vertical crack two-thirds of the way up. The descent gully, which meandered down one thousand feet of narrow, gravelly ledges next to Washington Column, was more dangerous than the wall itself. It was marked by faded slings fluttering on wizened shrubs that looked too thin to support a climber. They had been left behind by climbers who had lost their nerve and rappelled. Brian and David got to the top but only found the way down at twilight. Rather than take on the gully in the darkness, they made a fire and sat the night out.

In the morning, I wandered around camp, put on my shoes and climbed the slabby side of a giant boulder a couple of times. It never even occurred to me to organize a rescue for Brian and David. I had, as yet, little imagination for any of the things that could have gone wrong.

Instead of searching for my friends, I looked for a climbing partner in the parking lot of Yosemite Lodge, where climbers jangled slings of gear, gossiped and smoked pot. They soon dispersed to cliffs around the Valley, so I asked the only man left without a partner if he wanted to climb. Leaning against an old turquoise Ford truck, he stared at the sun through his shades as I spoke. After a silence that made me wonder if he had heard me, he introduced himself. Zeb had been to the Gunks and knew George, which showed how small the climbing world was. He said he wanted to try a 5.12, which was close to the top of the difficulty scale. He guessed it would be too hard for me, but to reach it, we would have to climb a 5.10 crack that he said would be a good introduction to Yosemite.

In Yosemite, most of the climbing started at 5.10, which at the time was a difficult grade. Zeb squirmed up the crack, and I struggled to follow. It was too narrow to chimney with the back on one side and feet on the other, and too wide to jam a fist or foot. Although I knew about techniques like stacking my hands on top of each other to jam a wide crack, I had never actually used them. I flailed, skinning my knees, elbows and hands on the crack's smooth walls. Waiting to figure things out in Yosemite wasn't working. On top, I lowered Zeb down his 5.12 crack and belayed him on a top-rope, and then we went home.

Driving back, Zeb complained that I had bungled the crack, but I needed no reminder. My lacerated hands stung. When I told him I planned to try the long prow of El Capitan, known as the Nose, he said I should choose an easier route. After he dropped me off in the parking lot, he tried to sell me some used climbing gear. My first day in the world's best rock climbing area had been a fiasco.

Back at camp, Brian and David told me about their ascent, but the bivouac and descent sounded more exciting than the climb. They planned a rest day drinking beer at a swimming hole. While they were still asleep the next morning, I looked for partners in the Camp Four parking lot. A few of the guys milling around there may have been climbers I'd seen in *Mountain*, but I couldn't be sure. They all had the same ponytails and tattered jean shorts.

One car with Ontario plates was owned by two climbers who knew nothing about Rattlesnake Point. They looked about my age but spoke a mixture of English and German that made them seem older. After buying the car in Toronto, they had driven it to the Gunks, Colorado and Yosemite because it was cheaper than flying all over the United States. Wolfgang Gullich was on his first trip outside of Europe. His partner, Ritchie, listed some of the extreme climbs they had done so far and asked if I had done them too. I explained that I climbed much less difficult routes, but they invited me to climb with them at the Cookie, a two-hundred-foot-high cliff famous for short, steep cracks.

An hour later, Ritchie belayed as I led a crack that was the perfect size for my hands. Waiting to work things out in Yosemite seemed a little less foolish now. From the belay ledge, Wolfgang led Butterballs, a finger-width 5.11 crack first climbed by Henry Barber. Wolfgang had climbed harder routes, but Ritchie said they usually climbed limestone at home in southern Germany and were still getting used to granite. Limestone was still unfashionable in America because it didn't readily succumb to the clean-climbing ethics popularized by Yosemite's Stonemasters. Wolfgang was already using the little farmland crags he climbed at in Germany as a laboratory for a new style of hard climbing that would change limestone's status, but at the time, the dominance of American granite was unquestioned.

In the car on the way back, the Germans sang along to a cassette tape of Hendrix, laughing as they Germanized some of the words.

Wolfgang did dozens of hard American climbs, including Separate Reality, a hand-sized slit in a thin flake of granite that extended 20 feet horizontally from an outcrop above the Cookie Cliff. Yosemite had several climbs named after Carlos Castaneda's books, but Separate Reality was the most unusual because you could see the sky through the crack while you were climbing. It was on the back cover of *Yosemite Climber*.

On that trip, I went to Separate Reality with Hugh Herr, who I knew from the Gunks. He had already climbed Astroman on Washington Column, a 1,100-foot-high 5.11 that might have been the hardest long free climb in the world. On Separate Reality, he slid cams into the crack and then flipped around the lip of the roof to hang down by his toes like a trapeze artist. A magazine said Hugh, at 15, was already the next great American rock climber. In 1982, however, when he was 18, he was caught in a winter storm on Mount Washington and rescued after a night in 30-below cold without bivouac gear. One of the rescuers died in an avalanche, and Hugh's frozen legs were amputated below the knees. Hugh's partner lost his lower left leg and right hand. Undefeated, Hugh climbed hard on homemade artificial limbs, earned a Ph.D. and became a professor of engineering at MIT, specializing in prosthetics.

Ten years later, I climbed Separate Reality and hoped I was strong enough for the Monument, a similar roof at White Bluff, on Georgian Bay. The Monument was eventually free climbed by Peter Croft, one of the finest rock climbers Canada ever produced. Around the same time, Wolfgang Gullich was filmed climbing Separate Reality without a rope. By then he had become the only person to ascend a 5.14 climb and soon set high standards on the rock walls of the Himalayas, Patagonia and the Alps. In 1992 he fell asleep at the wheel of his car on the Autobahn after doing an early morning radio interview and was killed; it was an unlikely end. Tearing down the road in an old car, singing along to Hendrix after a morning of hard climbing, 19-year-old Wolfgang had seemed indestructible.

After a few more days climbing short routes with anyone I could find, I was ready to try something longer. Even specialists in short climbs found it hard to resist the beauty of the thousand-foot routes that could be done in a day. A few all-day climbs supposedly readied me for a big wall, a climb that took more than a day to complete. This was, for me, the real reason I had gone to Yosemite, the quest I had hoped for since that dark night in the library basement, watching pictures of Yosemite's walls.

The realities of fulfilling that goal were mostly mundane. Hauling a duffel bag full of water, sleeping bags and food behind you, and then camping on a ledge or in a hammock, made big walls more exhausting and more committing than the mere difficulty of the climbing suggested. Even if you could do all of the climbing, which was typically slow aid climbing and steep free climbing, you could run out of food or water or become trapped by bad weather or an injury that might be minor on a small cliff but very serious on a big wall. Nonetheless, most Yosemite climbers hoped to climb at least one. My first big wall was the route I had seen in health class: the South Face of Washington Column. It was considered the easiest big wall in the Valley.

I had met my partner, Bill, in the Yosemite Lodge parking lot. I didn't know much about him, except that he came from Idaho and wanted to do some of the same climbs as me. I guessed he was five years my senior. I hoped he was more experienced than me and that his reticence was just modesty. Conversation was limited to what we were climbing, whether it was colder in Idaho or Canada, or how handguns were hard to get in Canada.

We dangled in webbing ladders, fought with ropes, fumbled with mechanical ascenders, struck thumbs with piton hammers, dropped several carabiners and hauled an unnecessarily heavy bag up Washington Column. On the afternoon of the second day, we pulled onto the top, where the air was oily with the scent of manzanitas. I wiped the sweat from my eyes with a hand grey with carabiner aluminum. My clumsy climbing had reminded me of my gym teacher's skepticism about my potential as a climber. I hadn't made it look easy, but I had learned that big walls are climbed not by daydreams but by painful inches.

Bill pointed down the Valley towards El Capitan. He made a gun barrel with his index finger and squinted, then slowly lowered his cocked thumb.

The Nose is a three-thousand-foot-high prow offering the easiest big-wall route on El Capitan. Although there was little climbing on the Nose that was harder than the South Face of Washington Column, it was three times as high. George had climbed the Nose in a day with Stonemaster Ron Kauk, but climbers like us took three days to get up it. A couple of big traverses made it tricky to rappel down if you lost your nerve or had an accident.

Preparing to make my first move on El Capitan from the gravelly ledges in the hot dawn twilight, my stomach twisted from the fumes of Bill's herbal cigarette. Washington Column had been over quickly enough that I hadn't had to adjust to its scale, but El Capitan was already different. The heat made the load of pitons and carabiners more oppressive. The knowledge that Dave had already climbed El Capitan was, if anything, discouraging, since he was a much better climber than me.

My greatest fear was that I would fail this test, that when the whistle blew and it was time to go over the top, I would be paralyzed by fear and fail. Would I come this far and simply have fate reject me when the landing-craft door came down? I kept climbing, and climbing proved that although I was not very brave, I was brave enough.

Hours passed, the sun moved across the wall and the updraft from the Valley's floor evaporated my first nervous sweat. I focused on what I could reach, shaking a piton or nut from the rack, placing or hammering it, weighting it slowly and gaining a foot, hoping it didn't rip out and send me flying. I was glad that Bill seemed unperturbed by the huge face and couldn't read my mind.

The next morning, I woke up sore from the ledge's bare rock and the harness I had slept in. Bill was chewing a piece of beef jerky and smoking. He said it was hard to sleep without a gun in the bedside drawer. He didn't feel safe. I remember his empty expression, the colour of the rope, the wisps of smoke. While I was asleep, he said, climbers who were moving so fast they might do the whole climb in a single day had passed like shadows.

Time on the wall diminished my fears. Expecting the carabiners, pitons and nuts tugging at my shoulders made them seem lighter. Coming second on my mechanical ascenders, I felt nothing when the rope stretched pencil-thin and twanged across overhangs a hundred feet above. On the third day, I welcomed the steepening climbing, since the bag hung free of the wall, making hauling easier.

The summit's granite pavement was split by a handful of stunted pines. Scabbed, bruised and thirsty, I lay in a rat's nest of our ropes and hardware. Bill looked across the Valley, whistling "Margaritaville" and pulling aluminum and blood-stained bandages from his hands. After our climb, he left Yosemite. For a climber like him, the Nose might have been the first of many big walls or a stepping stone to huge alpine walls. When I climbed in Idaho, a few years later, I asked about Bill in a climbing store, but the clerks didn't know him. I hope he went on to many great climbs.

I had done the easiest and most popular route on El Capitan. To put the Nose in perspective, it was climbed more than 20 times while I was in Yosemite that year, even though it wasn't the busiest season. Vancouver teenagers Hugh Burton and Steve Sutton had established two new routes on untravelled steep sections of El Capitan just a few years before. Neither of these difficult climbs saw a single attempt while I was in the Valley.

Even though my El Capitan climb was by the most common route, I had at least disproven George's prediction that I would die if I tried it, and passed the small test I had set for myself. It was neither my last big wall, nor the first of many. I wasn't patient enough for aid climbing. I was so clumsy with basic rope work that the technical wizardry serious big wallers use to crawl up acres of blank rock intimidated me. My first love was free climbs no longer than a rope-length, after which came longer routes I could free climb. On the day after the Nose, however, I felt like a real big-wall climber and drew my route on a postcard of El Capitan for Judy.

The clerk at the post office saw my name and said I had a letter in general delivery. Hoping that it was from a girl I knew, even though I knew it could not be, I opened it. A woman asked me to come home to Oregon soon. She missed me and would have to give up the apartment because she couldn't make the rent on her own. If I was making enough money at the lodge, could I send her some? Anyway, even if I was broke, I should come home. They were hiring again at the mill. Deflated, I folded it up and left it at the post office for the man at the lodge with the same name as me. I was disappointed with how much I had wanted someone else's praise for passing a test that, after all, I had kept largely to myself.

That night we were a little quieter while drinking the last

of our Rusty Nail supply. In the morning, we loaded the car, leaving only a couple of Drambuie and whisky empties on the picnic table. El Capitan's reversed image disappeared in the rear-view mirror.

In the early evening, we pulled into a truck stop in the Nevada desert so David could call his wife. A man in the diner asked where I was from. He had assumed that Brian's licence was a novelty plate from Ontario, California. "Canada" – he repeated the word. He said he might go up there now that he had gambled and lost a house, wife, kids, everything. He asked if I was a gambler. I said I wasn't, but my grandfather gambled. It runs in the blood, he warned me. I should remember him. He looked at the ground and just said, "Well," as if I'd discouraged him in some way.

Shirtless and gaunt, Brian sat in the car and sang along with a country tune on the radio until David came back from the phone booth. David's wife had told him that George's party on the Cassin Ridge on Denali hadn't been seen for two weeks. The first week, the rangers said they might be lost on one of the vast glaciers. By the second week, they were confident the men had died in an avalanche. Brian swore and turned off the radio.

When I was five years old, I was playing on the floor in a pool of sunlight when my mother told me that my father's mother had died. Her death ended decades of lung problems caused by chain-smoking, but to me it was sudden. My mother said she was with the angels, and the sunlight shining through the window brightened a little, as if to prove she was right.

That winter a climber who had been on Denali during the accident wrote in the *American Alpine Journal*: "I talked with four Toronto climbers who were starting for the Cassin. Late in August, I learned these climbers were never seen again, undoubtedly victims of an avalanche." After the accident, the crevasse-ridden, avalanche-swept East Fork of the Kahiltna Glacier where they disappeared became known as the Valley of Death.

How devoid of frailty they had sometimes seemed. Not just George Manson, but also Al Chase and Sean Lewis. I had met Al just once, before he left Yosemite for Alaska. He had lost his rock shoes but climbed the difficult three-hundred-foot Serenity Crack barefoot and shirtless. I usually saw Sean at Buffalo Crag, where, in just a headband, shorts and rock shoes, he did most of his climbing alone, without a rope. He once told me how he had fallen out of a hammock halfway up a big wall and woke up when the rope tied around his waist caught him.

So, in the summer of 1979, when I was 16, me and a few other suburban misfits were left with most of the harder climbs and the small, steep, out-of-the-way crags to ourselves. Climbers who we had admired and tried to emulate lay in graves more lonely and mysterious than those of exiled poets. The precise day it happened will never be known, but death had been discriminating in its choice of victims. The four men had no monument besides the name their deaths gave to the place they were buried. I only knew the dead men for a little while, but perhaps a name that is a warning is the kind of memorial George, in any case, would have liked.

CHAPTER 9

Jokers

A few days later, a teacher handing me textbooks saw the crack scabs on my hands and warned me against fighting in school. I was back at Etobicoke Collegiate for Grade 12, the second-last grade for anyone whose parents thought they were bound for university. The only change to my schoolwork was that I wrote my essays in the slangy, journalistic style enjoined by the writing books Gerry Banning gave me. It didn't improve my marks.

If I skipped school to climb, I was always caught. The vice-principal sensed rebellion, but there was little he could do. I intended to waste my youth on climbing. He warned me that I would have miserable jobs and gain glory only in something few valued or understood, that I would fall in with knaves and in the end have nothing to show for the years except my experiences. Some of this happened, but he was wrong when he said it wouldn't be worth it.

I fell to the bottom of the school hierarchy. Stoners sitting on the hoods of other people's cars asked me for a light. Tina's brother, who had seen William fall from the bridge, speculated that I only climbed because I was on drugs and asked if I could get him some. When I explained that I wasn't, that I just liked to climb, he said I must be a psycho. I sensed a compliment.

There were others who were more committed to climbing than I was. Dave accepted poverty as the price of his devotion to climbing. His girlfriend was back in Toronto, and when I visited them she set out tea cups on a crate with a towel as a tablecloth. With a cigarette in one hand and a beer in the other, Dave ignored the tea and raved about climbing.

His favourite subject was moving to Yosemite; the Gunks; Boulder, Colorado, or some other centre of the climbing world. George, with his headbands and summers in Yosemite, had connected Rattlesnake Point to the wider climbing world. After his death, the little group that had surrounded him dispersed. Rob moved to the Rockies. After a couple of years, Mike went out west on an extended climbing trip interrupted by winters working on ski lifts. Tom lingered a while before going home to the US.

Dave wanted to leave too, but couldn't afford it. Talent fuelled Dave's desire to be a great climber. His mentor's death, trouble with his girlfriend and more than usually demeaning jobs made it hard for him to find fulfillment in the flat world. When his girlfriend moved to Montreal again, he started drifting between the Gunks, Toronto and Montreal.

Sig, Pete and Reg started climbing later than me and missed George's heyday at Rattlesnake. The accident in Alaska therefore scarcely affected them. After the wild ride of his first climbing season, Reg had developed a little caution to back up his ability to hang on to small holds for a long time. A summer climbing with Sig, Pete and Dave had built his repertoire of movement and showed him life-saving tricks with equipment. When I left, Reg was climbing his first hard routes. When I returned, he had done dozens of them.

Sig and Reg had started to climb together. Reg was brash and Sig was a loner, but these differing traits compelled them both to occasional extremes on the rock. Twice in the space of an hour, Reg walked below a climb Sig was soloing before asking why he hadn't moved. Sig said he was stuck and couldn't hold on much longer. Reg rushed to the top with a rope and rescued him. Sig's shyness was stronger than his fear of death; he wouldn't ask climbers he didn't know for help.

Some saw courting death on just-beyond-the-suburbs outcrops as an evolutionary dead end for climbing; risks, if taken, should be saved for the great ranges. But these were the rocks that had drawn us to climbing, and we weren't saving our lives for something else. I was a little surprised that Yosemite hadn't made me feel differently about my native limestone landscape. I began to understand how British climbers who fought their way up Himalayan faces also obsessed about 30-foot outcrops in their home counties.

Judy and I went to a slideshow where the new edition of Jim Mark's Ontario rock-climbing guidebook was released. Written with his usual panache, and complete in its coverage of the popular cliffs of Bon Echo and Rattlesnake Point, it also made a strange concession to the free-climbing trend by dropping all aid ratings in the list of Mount Nemo's routes. Climbs graded 5.7 A1, which might have been 5.10 or harder if free climbed, were rated 5.7. It was a frustrating error for a young climber bent on free climbing old aid climbs. There were no actual descriptions of how to find and climb the routes at Mount Nemo, even though it was the highest and longest cliff close by. It seemed like Mark simply didn't think enough people climbed there to bother researching and describing the climbs. Like all guidebook writers, he played a role in creating climbing communities by directing climbers towards well-described cliffs and away from those he omitted. Since the only usably complete information was for Bon Echo and Rattlesnake Point (and the distant and tiny Kingston Mills), most of the climbers went to those cliffs. My disappointment that he had included neither the old climbs of Mount Nemo nor the hard new climbs George and his friends had done at newly explored cliffs led me to start taking notes on the climbs that I did. I hoped to one day write a complete guidebook to the limestone crags I had known since I was a child on McGillivray's Hill and fallen in love with when I had become a climber. I eventually wrote five guidebooks, and I have Jim Mark to thank for inspiring me.

I purchased a copy of the new guidebook, but Judy didn't need one. She had been accepted at McGill, which, as she had said, was closer to the Gunks and Val-David than to the escarpment. Not that she would be climbing much; university and her spiritual hobbies would take up most of her time.

In Judy's house there was a photo of her as a red-cheeked little girl beside a silver-tinselled Christmas tree. She was wide-eyed, anticipating the blessing of gifts. She loved her family and enjoyed their support, but by the time she was a young woman, she wanted better answers than the make-believe of childhood. In Judy's 17th year, when I introduced myself to her at SEE, she began sleeping in tents, climbing, doing yoga, meditating, practicing vegetarianism, reading about Eastern spirituality, smoking dope and falling in love. Hers was a thoroughly new life.

My need for change was met more simply by scrambling through cane brush and mossy boulders with my climbing friends, in search of cliffs I had never seen. We sometimes left behind pitons or slings on new climbs, partly to make the routes easier if we came back and partly just to mark our efforts. Driving home, we argued over whether to name the routes we had just put up after girls, daydreams or rock songs.

Although such outcrops usually had no good established climbs, George's Fearless Warrior at the secluded Cow Crag was an exception. Climbing the startlingly thin crack was part elegy, part rite of passage. Holding on and twiddling wired nuts into the crack, my concentration was clouded by memories of the dead man who had first done it. Here, the worlds of the living and the dead converged.

We accorded George, who we had known only a little, a kind of respect we denied to a more permanent custodian of climbing: the Toronto Section of the Alpine Club. Although without the section's initial exploration – naming and grading routes and recording them in a guidebook – none of us would have been able to pursue climbing as we did, our wildness and indifference put us naturally at odds with some of the section's civility and cautiousness.

This was most apparent at Bon Echo. In the early climbing days there, in the 1960s, the cliff had seen some aggressive climbers; Dave started climbing at Bon Echo just as they were retiring. He once accompanied a white-haired gentleman on an unroped ascent of the ridge on which William and I had had our epic. The man drank from a wineskin as he climbed. Near the top, he laughed and said he was "sleeping." Dave assumed he was taking a nap on a ledge, but he wasn't; he was slipping. On their vacations, climbers like Dave's partner tore up big climbs in Yosemite and the Alps. By my time, they had gone, and most visitors used the hut as a cook shack for tranquil weekends, doing the odd climb, swimming in the lake or reading on the hut veranda.

There were few rules at the hut. The main ones were phoning ahead so you could be picked up at the marina, bringing a tent and paying a small fee. We seldom called ahead, often slept in the hut instead of our own tents and were usually too broke to pay fees. After neglecting to call to get picked up, a young climber stole a boat and drove it across the lake to the hut, intending to return it the next day. In the morning, the police spotted the stolen vessel at the club dock. Clubmen not in the habit of breaking laws said it wouldn't happen again.

The boat theft wasn't repeated, but the other sources of tension multiplied. At a late-night party, I fell off the porch. Dave hammered a piton between the porch boards to anchor me until an understandably groggy man came over and told him to stop. He started hammering again as soon as the old man was back in his tent. There were tightrope-walking contests on boards nailed between trees for pull-ups. Beach chairs were unfolded on the hut roof for drinking sessions. Ghetto blasters were abused. The rules for cooking times were ignored. Reg brought a small-gauge shotgun and a skeet trap and shot clay pigeons from the dock at night.

The climbing logbook in the hut became a battleground. Dave made a free ascent of an old aid climb and recorded it in the logbook with a new route name. When someone crossed it out, Dave wrote in an even more outrageous route name. When this too was censored, he stopped recording his routes in the book and started using it to kill mice.

Reg, Dave and their friends often visited on weekdays, when the hut and cliff were empty. Like aristocrats who held weekday shooting parties to exclude anyone responsible enough to have a real job, they took advantage of the solitude to climb as they pleased – sometimes unroped in the moonlight – drink in the afternoons and hold pull-up or knife-throwing competitions. Their parties were interrupted by serious climbs, like the first free ascent of Compulsion, a steep and difficult climb that George had said would never be climbed without hanging on pitons. They also repeated some of the hard climbs done by George's group, many of which were, ironically, harder than Compulsion.

Little groups of young climbers we didn't know had begun to show up at the Milton cliffs, where we mainly ignored each other. But at Bon Echo, where we camped, ate and went to the cliff together in the boat, new friendships and rivalries were unavoidable.

A group from Hamilton swelled the hut's biota of young hard climbers. Chas Yonge, an English graduate student at McMaster University, was the most experienced and, although only in his early 20s, the oldest. He had a goatee, great technique and a wicked sense of humour. He often climbed with teenagers John Kaandorp and Peter Zabrok, who I had met at Rattlesnake and ice climbing in a gorge outside Hamilton. In winter John had worn a green janitor's jacket, steel-toed boots and workman's gloves, and he chipped footholds in a frozen waterfall with a carpenter's hammer. Peter wore thick, fogged glasses and had a carabiner. I didn't forget them, because I knew how motivated men with improvised climbing gear could be. Chas also knew how ambitious they were. He once had to phone John's mother to assure her John was being safe, although the jokes he told us about making the call post-mortem made his sincerity seem dubious.

"John will be a little late for dinner today. Very late actually. Well, to be honest, he won't be coming home at all. He died climbing today. Yes, I know, we're not surprised either. Sorry, cheerio."

It was years before John's gear was all legitimate. Even when he climbed 5.10, John passed the rope through a loop of webbing around his legs before tying it around his waist with a bowline. The rig looked more desperate and, in the event of a fall, painful, than just tying the rope around his waist. Bulging muscles from endless buildering circuits in Hamilton, and an obsession with doing new climbs with a minimum of protection, confirmed Chas Yonge's comment that he had "the devil up his ass." With Peter Zabrok and Steve De Maio from nearby Burlington, they put up scores of new routes without bolts, pitons or even cleaning off loose rock. Steve later helped put up some of the hardest, most dangerous rock climbs in the Rockies. Even after Peter climbed dozens of hard El Capitan routes, he said that John Kaandorp was more single-mindedly devoted to climbing than anyone else he knew.

Like us they were a cohesive little group who probably interpreted the forbearance of mature climbers like Brian Hibbert and Chas Yonge as admiration. Also like us, they came from the mushrooming suburbs.

The first climber our age we knew who didn't come from the suburbs was Arnold. He had been at a private school that boasted a program of corporal punishment and gruelling wilderness trips. On one excursion, 12 students and a teacher drowned in a canoe accident. The school said it was better for kids to die in the woods than in front of a television. Not a single parent sued. Having learned the law of the jungle, Arnold quit school to live by it. He wasn't much older than me, but the two most important things in his life had just happened. He had moved in with an older woman and had just finished a beginner climbing course.

At first sight he looked like a redneck, with his green down vest, bandana and thin teenage beard. Within minutes of meeting us, he pointed at a steep crack, asking Dave Lanman if it was easy and if he had done it. It was moderately difficult and Dave had soloed it, but he just shrugged and said Arnold should try it if he really wanted to know. Given Dave's usual tendency to push people onto hard climbs, I sensed a

warning, but Arnold didn't know Dave. With borrowed carabiners and slings, Arnold climbed to some pitons 20 feet up,
ran out of strength, jumped and landed unhurt beside a knife-
edged boulder that could have split him in two.

"Just testing the landing," he said. It was his first attempt
at lead climbing.

I had no one to climb with at Bon Echo the next weekend,
and Arnold's show of dash suggested that he might be enthusiastic. Partway up our first climb at Bon Echo, he struggled
into the sling with the protection and asked for a refresher
on how nuts worked. I showed him how a couple of standard
pieces of gear fit in cracks. Fifty feet above me, he stretched
out his arm with a fistful of hexagonal nuts.

"You forgot to tell me about these. Think they'd work up
here?"

At the belay ledge, I told him that the protection was
poorly placed. He said he had placed it that way so he could
move quickly. When I said it would rip out if he fell, he
laughed.

He dropped me off in the city and asked for ten bucks
for gas and another ten for wear and tear on his girlfriend's
car. I gave him a ten-dollar bill. He had moved back into his
parents' house in Rosedale, one of the wealthiest neighbourhoods in Toronto, and was free to devote himself to getting
stronger and ticking off harder climbs.

Dave's climbing on Bon Echo's often lichen-covered, loose, hard-to-protect rock startled some and induced others to try to do the same. He had learned a lot there with George, with whom he had made the first ascent of the most difficult route on the cliff. When, shirtless and sunburnt, beer in hand, he twisted the clutch on the boat's outboard until the engine screamed but the boat went no faster, he seemed more carefree than he did anywhere else. There was, however, something a little haunted about how the boat often ended up beneath a particular unfinished climb he had started with George. It began at Thunder Crack, a 50-foot high fissure rising straight from the water, but was halted higher up by a man-killing flake that quivered when it was touched but could not be safely dislodged from below.

One afternoon Dave was pointing at the unstable stone and guessing how to bypass it. Sig, Reg and I, who had all tried the climb with Dave and failed because George had been right and the rock was too loose, sat amidships. In the bow were Arnold and the teenage daughters of an older climber. Arnold asked Dave if he had ever soloed a 5.9. Dave said no, although he had soloed at a level that Arnold hadn't even climbed with a rope. He wasn't paying attention, hoping, perhaps, to change the subject to his unfinished climb, or girls or booze.

Undaunted, Arnold pointed to Thunder Crack and asked if he had soloed that. Dave shook his head, smiling at the girls.

Arnold laced up his climbing shoes. He stepped out of the boat onto the cliff confidently, but 20 feet up, his left foot slipped on some sooty lichen and he lost his nerve. After one last look upwards, he waved to Dave to bring the boat beneath him. Dave told him he could make it if he relaxed, which was his solution to all climbing problems. Arnold cursed and jumped into the lake. As he pulled himself over the gunwales, dripping like a wet Labrador, Dave said the route should be renamed Voyage to the Bottom of the Sea, after the television series about submarines.

We dropped Arnold off that night after wheedling a couple of dollars for gas out of him. Sig asked him for food in exchange for wear and tear on Reg's car, but Arnold slammed the front door behind him.

Remembering that Arnold still had a piece of his equipment, Reg knocked on the door. No one answered, so he went round the back of the house, where, through a kitchen window, he saw Arnold carving a roast chicken. It was six o'clock, so Reg and I would get no food at home. My father's dinner was served at precisely 5:30 – too early to get back after a climbing day – and if you missed it, the alternative was, at best, a peanut butter sandwich. Sig was always hungry and had become a relentless scrounger.

Reg called Sig over. When he saw Arnold eating, Sig burst through the back door, jostling an elderly man who could have been a butler or Arnold's father, and grabbed the food.

They ran back to the car, and we squealed out of the driveway while Sig laughed and tore off a chicken leg.

Arnold now tried even harder to gain some level of respect, although his reluctance to travel made this difficult. He had been to a couple of areas within a day's drive but preferred his home crags. He mainly limited himself to Rattlesnake Point, where his exploits would at least be seen, although not by the climbers he wanted to impress, who found steep, out-of-the-way little outcrops more relevant. The growing number of climbers who had visited spectacular faraway climbing areas also deflected attention from Arnold's achievements. He knew, however, that there was a means to advance his reputation without driving to California or labouring on new routes. Bon Echo, the highest cliff in his ambit, offered a chance at pre-eminence. The problem was that he would risk his life if he free soloed the Joke.

The Joke is a steep black wall leading to a narrow ramp stuck to the side of the cliff like a busted shelf. It had first been climbed in 1961, a year before I was born, by John Turner. Turner was the author of Sweet Dreams, the climb I had done with Norbert on my first visit. Before he succeeded, Turner took two big falls on the Joke. The first broke one of his legs, and the second put him in the lake. The Joke was the only Ontario climb mentioned in Jones's magisterial history, *Climbing in North America*. Jones called it "unrelenting."

Everyone I climbed with, including Arnold, had done

the Joke. At 5.9, it wasn't especially difficult, but the long distances between protection cracks, especially at the crux, made it a rite of passage for serious climbers. Alone and rope-less, however, its grade would be an uncountable number. Its beauty belied sections of friable rock and cruxes that would be chancy to climb back down if you lost your nerve. A hand-ful of difficult Bon Echo climbs had been free soloed, but the Joke remained. Reg's love of risk was exuberant but not mor-bid, and he wouldn't touch it. Sig considered it. Dave Lanman could have done it easily, since he had soloed 5.10 and 5.11 climbs at Bon Echo. He knew it would be awesome, he just didn't think it would be fun.

At school I had daydreamed I was high on the Joke with no rope when I mistook a piece of lichen for a foothold. My foot twitched and I started, grabbing at an imaginary hand-hold and knocking my notebook off my desk. The teacher stopped talking for a moment, asked if I was all right and carried on as I picked up my book, my heart beating like a swallow's. The accident on the Cassin Ridge had made me re-consider whether all my good luck was still ahead of me, as I had assumed it was last season. If George Manson wasn't im-mortal, neither was I.

Arnold proved that his sense of immortality was still healthy by free soloing the climb that we all feared or avoided. From the top, he scrambled down to the lake and swam to the canoe he had left at the bottom of the climb. Petroglyphs of rock spirits who ate the souls of the impure gazed blankly at the young warrior as he paddled home. So did Dave when he heard about it.

Gerry Banning said Arnold had been driven to it by our reverse class discrimination. Whatever Arnold wanted from climbing, he had found soloing the Joke, and afterwards he climbed less. When I got a ride to climb at Mount Nemo with Gerry and Arnold that fall, I didn't know that neither of them really wanted to climb that day, and that it would be the last time I saw Arnold.

Mount Nemo was dark, sometimes loose and as isolated as the local climbing could be. Brian Hibbert had done some first ascents there and had showed me a long crack splitting an overhang. Old pitons saved me from placing nuts at the crux and made it easier to be the first to climb it using just the holds on the rock. I had made first ascents before – my first climb, on a shale riverbank, was probably a first ascent – but this was a new route that was good enough for someone else to do.

When I went to Nemo with Gerry and Arnold, I hoped to try an unclimbed crack I had seen, but partway there, they detoured to a doughnut store. I looked out the window at vultures circling above the crags as Arnold and Gerry ate their doughnuts.

"You shouldn't let climbing become an addiction or another job," said Gerry.

"It's all about balance," said Arnold, sucking purple jelly out of a doughnut. "That's what I learned on the Joke." He caught my eye for a second. "Solo."

He was making a point that didn't matter to me. I wasn't searching for balance, just for improved climbing technique.

The next time I saw Gerry, he was angry. He had loaned Arnold his car and when it broke down partway to the Gunks, Arnold ditched it and phoned Gerry for money for the bus for the rest of the trip. The last thing I remember hearing he was doing in the climbing community was building a sauna at Bon Echo. In 2014 I heard a rumour that he had left for Africa to hang out on the beach and do some sailing. I like to imagine him lounging by the fire under the Southern Cross, sharing with the other beach dwellers the story of how the Joke was soloed.

CHAPTER 10

Avenue des Pins

Judy and I pitched a tent between the emerald-leaved birches. Rain had soaked us while we crossed the cold water of Mazinaw Lake. Mike Tschipper, who I wouldn't see again for years after this weekend, grimaced as water poured through a hole he had punched in a garbage bag for his head. Judy and I had our own source of misery. It was June 1980, and we were fighting about our plans for the next year.

In the summer, I would teach rock climbing to fund a trip to Yosemite with Brian Hibbert, Reg and Gerry Banning. In the fall, I would be free from school. Reg and Sig wanted to work in oil- and job-rich Alberta and then head to the Mojave Desert and Yosemite to climb in the spring. When I told Judy I was considering going with them, she said I was squandering my life. We'd been over it before. For her, climbing was an opportunity for education, travel and personal growth, but for me, it was just a path to more climbing.

The next morning we joined the climbers in the boat bound for a route we could both do easily. As we passed the Joke, however, Judy said that this was her last trip to Bon Echo and she wanted to climb it. She looked serious as she tightened her harness buckle. I didn't tell her about the traverse where a fall, even seconding, could hurt her, I just grabbed my rope and rack and told the boatman to take us in.

On a tiny, wet ledge we tied in to the same rope for the last time. Judy watched nervously as I led up steep, dark rock to a menacingly protruding piton, but I wasn't worried: I had done the climb before. Even dangerous climbs lose much of their terror when the holds and exact places for protection are known. The crux traverse started at a slanting overhang 60 feet above the lake. The hardest moves were close to the protection, and I began to enjoy the rock, the smell of chalk on sweaty fingertips and the feel of tight rock shoes on tiny holds.

There was, however, little protection for the climber coming second. From the belay, the rope swooped down across the face to Judy, who had climbed the crux and was inching towards me. Just as she reached the safety of the ramp, her fingers popped off the face and she swung out of sight. The rope zipped across the edge of the ramp, sending tufts of nylon flying. She had disproven the myth that if the second climber fell at that point, the rope would cut on the ramp, but she now hung free of the rock. She yelled that she was going to use the thin climbing line lacing her shoes to tie prusik knots and climb the rope.

Prusiking took a long time because the knots tightened when weighted and had to be loosened before being pushed upwards again. When Judy finally got to the ledge, she was breathing hard, her hair was damp with sweat and her knuckles were bloody. She tried to smile and seem ready to go on. We did go on, but after the intensity of the first pitch, the rest of the climb was almost a relief.

On top, lightning flashed in black clouds and thunder cracked in the forest. I dropped the equipment on the rock and Judy stumbled a little as she took off her harness. Heat mingled with the smells of sweat and junipers.

"I just wanted to do something hard to remember being here," she said. "I didn't mean to fall."

Drops of rain became a torrent and sluiced down the rocks and through the junipers. We huddled together for a few minutes on a slab until it passed. The descent gully was still streaming as we lowered ourselves down roots and ledges to the lake.

A.J. Casson's painting of Mazinaw Rock captures the massive grey and pink ridges of ancient granite transected by the dark face dropping to cold water. A reproduction hangs above my fireplace now. Defying the dull, art nouveau sunlight, a stone ridge glows bone white above a flicker of stone ramp. Casson took some liberties with the shape of the cliff a climber might not, but it occurs to me when I see this painting that his bright ridge is more or less the top of the Joke, where Judy and I once waited in the storm.

On the way home from Bon Echo on the weekend we climbed the Joke, I said I was going to climb the CN Tower the next morning. I had put off telling her because I worried she would see it as a sign that my obsession with climbing was no longer limited to rocks. She said it was hare-brained enough to be the kind of thing I would do, but the caper had actually been planned by Gerry Banning. I just had to show up and climb.

I would learn Gerry's motive for the climb later, but mine could be summed up in the much-quoted words of George Mallory: because it was there. In mountain cities, you could see mountains from downtown, so people thought about climbing them. In Toronto they built the world's highest tower, and it also begged to be climbed. The mile-high pinnacle of concrete stuck out of the railway yards where my mother had played as a child but was visible in faraway Etobicoke. It shone with the silicone of enough crushed escarpment rock to build a small city. Some of the rock came from the quarry behind Cow Crag, where dust coated the holds after dynamiting.

Class had been suspended to watch TV coverage of a Sikorsky helicopter installing the antenna on the tower's summit. We were told that the tower was a gift to the city and nation from the Canadian National Railway Company. Construction began in 1973, when the CBC broadcast a TV series on how companies like CN had laid the railways that had united the country. The tower was both patriotic and commercial. Downtown skyscrapers were too low to broadcast the TV signals that were the lifeblood of commerce and culture. The signal sent from the CN Tower, however, would reach the TV antennae of every metastasizing suburb.

As kids, Reg and I loved the monster movies broadcast by Buffalo TV stations but could only watch them at my paternal cousins' because they had a 30-foot aluminum antenna mast and we didn't. We sat awestruck on their vinyl couch as Greek heroes fought skeletons and King Kong climbed the Empire State Building to swat biplanes. After the movie, our cousins dared Reg and me to climb their TV mast like King Kong. As the mast swayed in the summer wind curling around the cul-de-sac, we saw across miles of rooftops to the tower rising above black office buildings.

We knew you didn't have to be King Kong to climb a skyscraper. In 1977 New York climber George Willig climbed the World Trade Center in New York City. It had briefly been a national news story. Gerry Banning discovered that an ascent of the CN Tower would be much easier than Willig's climb. Window frames projecting a hand's width every three feet made a ladder of holds, and a metal rail offered another grip. Bolts sticking out of the metal could be used as protection. Gerry had made bolt hangers out of nylon webbing slings with loops sealed with electrical tape and hardware-store washers glued to wing nuts. Actual climbing bolt hangers would have been safer, but they weren't available in Toronto. With Gerry's hangers and regular climbing gear, we could clamber up the window frames, stopping to belay every 150 feet. Passing the massive observation and restaurant pod would require drilling holes in the tower, so Gerry decided to stop at the top of the windows.

A phone call to the fire department revealed that their longest ladder wouldn't reach from the parking lot to the tower. A tourist brochure bragged that the wind-proof windowpanes could only be removed with special machinery, so they couldn't be opened to nab us. The window-cleaning platform was stored off-site and took a day to assemble and thus was no threat, since Gerry estimated the climb would only take a few hours. Gerry chose to climb on the tower's fifth anniversary, June 23, 1980. The T-shirts he had made "said happy birthday cn tower."

Judy dropped me at Gerry's, and I lay awake on a couch suffused with decades of dope smoke. I struggled to believe the plan was real. My parents thought I was still at Bon Echo, but starting the climb from their house would have been impossible. The first they would hear about it was when Reg phoned them the next morning.

Before dawn, we put on our harnesses and piled into Reg's car with our gear. It was still dark when we ran up the stairs and across the plaza to the tower's north side, which Gerry had chosen partly so the whole city could see us. We scrambled unroped for about 30 feet and started rigging the first belay. Reg rushed to a pay phone to call the newspapers and radio stations, hoping to collect cash prizes for the best news tip of the day. A security guard caught us in his flashlight beam and ordered us down. Gerry told him the details were in a press release he'd left on the ground. Soon the sun was up and a small crowd gathered below. Front Street, across the railway tracks, was jammed with cars full of commuters trying to see us. Police cars and ambulances filled the tower parking lot. Reg stood in front of a TV camera and talked into a reporter's microphone.

The first three rope-lengths got us about four hundred feet up. The bolt hangers were easy to use, and the climbing was simple but draining because it was vertical and repetitive. I asked Gerry to lead. He said if he had to lead, we'd just have to go down, then handed me a plastic bottle sloshing with brown fluid. "It's herbal tea," he said, "to help you recover."

I had expected Gerry to want to lead part of the climb he had planned. He explained, however, that he hadn't come up to lead climb but to prove that he wasn't like his father. He looked scared. I wasn't angry; after all, if it hadn't been for him, I wouldn't have been there at all.

At five hundred feet, my own father appeared on the other side of the glass. He looked frustrated. It's hard, after all, to imagine a good way to handle being put in his position. Next to him, a man in a suit pointed downwards and shouted. Ted from the Alpine Club was trying to calm him down. The thick glass muffled the suit's words. He said they couldn't open the windows to let us in and asked me what I was doing. I said we didn't need the window open and climbed out of view, but the encounter had affected me. In the far west I thought I could see the escarpment: a long limestone ripple in the flat carpet of farmland. I suddenly felt that I wasn't climbing, I was performing a stunt.

Reporters photographed us through the window as we rappelled. The next morning, for the first and last time, the front page of the newspapers showed a young man hanging from a harness, wearing dirty white pants and climbing hardware, his shoulder-length hair held back with a handkerchief. Now I think I looked a little ridiculous, but I heard that at the time it inspired some young climbers in the area.

A squad car took us to a downtown police station. Cops who usually busted drug dealers and pimps cheered as we were brought to a room with chairs bolted to the floor. The station chief yelled at us and made us promise never to climb another building in Toronto again, and we were released. Gerry beamed as he chatted with the newsmen outside.

On the drive home, my father said that what I had done

took nerve, even if he couldn't understand it. He was worried, however, about my mother, who had spent the morning in a state of anguish stoked by her friend Dorcas. When I got home, my mother staggered to her feet, although Dorcas told her she was in no condition to get up and that it was all my fault and that I was lucky my mother hadn't dropped dead from shame. I was glad that this was the only time her and Dorcas actually saw me climb. I felt sorry for my mother, because although the climb had never really been dangerous, it had upset her. I didn't feel the same way about Dorcas.

Judy called me that night. She was as surprised as I was by the events of the day, but was too busy studying for her last, Grade-13, high-school exam to see me. The vice-principal said he wanted to punish me but couldn't because the CN Tower was off school property and the school year was almost over. Expulsion was certain if I ever climbed the school building. Next year he expected to see a difference in me. I didn't tell him that I had climbed the school several times and that the empty booze bottles I found on the roof proved I hadn't made the first ascent. I also hoped to see a difference in myself next year, although not the one he was hoping for.

He told me to see the guidance counsellor, but I never did. I just didn't understand people who found suburbia liveable without something like climbing. I was tired of having to explain myself.

Eight weeks later, I was with Brian Hibbert on the overhanging plane of Yosemite's Leaning Tower. The climbing was easy but strenuous, exposed and slow. From the bivouac ledge, I watched stars come out and tiny lights of stoves and headlamps flicker from ledges and hammocks on El Capitan. A year before, one of those little lights had been mine. The year before that, one had been George's. Back then, I had worn a headband and white pants, like George and the California climbers in magazines. This second Valley year, I showed up as myself, in a dirty but efficient baseball cap, threadbare canvas trousers cut off below the knees and T-shirts I wore until they fell apart.

I took my place among the tribes of climbers who had come from even farther away than my own home crags. Japanese climbers proudly showed me crack scabs like they were duelling scars. Ghastly thin Brits with pockmarked skin asked about El Capitan in Oxbridge accents. There were hippie Germans and Australians with punk hairdos. Cowboys from cliffs in Wyoming, Oklahoma and Texas distrusted the Australians. Southerners who drove barefoot whooped as they threw themselves at the walls. Some of the best climbers came from cliffs in Oregon few had heard of.

Gerry Banning, Reg and Sig Isaac came to Yosemite with us that summer. Their first route was a nine-hundred-foot vertical wall. Although the guidebook said it was at a difficulty Sig and Reg had climbed all day in the Gunks, they conservatively planned to take two days.

The author, Morphine Ledge, Mount Nemo, Ontario, 1978. Headband, Whillans harness, thick rope and jamming tape were all the rage for '70s rock climbers. (Personal Collection)

Climbing hardman, straight shooter, truck driver and bandana fan George Manson, Rattlesnake Point, Ontario, 1978. (Chris Rogers)

Mike Tschipper
at Bon Echo,
Ontario, 1977.
(Chris Rogers)

Judy Paddon hitchhiking to Chapel
Pond, Adirondacks, 1978.
(Courtesy Jamie Paddon)

Steve Labelle, the first
climber I met, climb-
ing the flat side of
the Separate Reality
roof, Yosemite, 1978.
(Richard Massiah
Collection)

Dave Lanman around the
time I first met him, ca.
1978. (Richard Massiah
Collection)

Gerry Banning at Rattlesnake Point, 1979. (Gerry Banning Collection)

Brian Hibbert on iconic '70s route Space Case, Rattlesnake Point, 1980.
(Reg Smart III Collection)

Reg Smart on Popeye, at Bon Echo, 1980, with a full complement of '70s rock gear, including nuts that have fallen out of the crack. (Reg Smart III Collection)

Sig Isaac (sitting on hood) and Reg Smart, with the car Reg bought with his Katimavik money at Six Points in Toronto, in Hidden Valley Campground, Joshua Tree National Monument, southern California, 1981. (Reg Smart III Collection)

Unfortunately they drank most of the water slogging up to the cliff and came back without climbing a foot. After a couple of shorter climbs, Gerry discovered Yosemite's restaurants, pools, shops and lounges and spent as much of his trip in his Speedo as he did in his climbing harness. As a team of two, Reg and Sig were able to chase their dreams more ruthlessly.

Previously, Reg had been Sig's second choice as climbing partner, after Pete Reilly, but Pete had stayed in Toronto. Although Sig and Pete would visit Yosemite together in the future, the end of high school had changed things for now. Pete went to university, married, bought a house and started a career before these things meant much, or were even possible, for the rest of us.

Reg's exuberance made Pete's adulthood seem premature. Reg's luck seemed to blot out fear. He was often injured in après-climbing parties, but almost never on the rock. He and Sig climbed climbed thousands of feet of granite, suffering little more than a few crack scabs, and learning as they went. When Reg left, Sig soloed Washington Column, his first big wall.

Soloing a big wall is not free soloing. There is no breezy trade of safety for freedom from equipment and rope protocols. The solo big-wall climber must use a sketchy self-belay system, lead the pitch, rappel it, release the haul bag, climb the rope with mechanical ascenders and remove all the equipment, then haul up the bag. It's a kind of climbing full of suffering so totally private that afterwards it's almost as if it had never happened. It was easy to see how soloing a big wall made Sig feel paid up in several of his bleaker philosophical tendencies. A year later, he soloed Leaning Tower. On the bivouac ledge, he untied from the anchor to organize a rope and threw a haul bag with his water in it off the ledge to make room. In a flash, he remembered that it wasn't tied in. Let it go, or grab it and risk being pulled into an eight-hundred-foot free fall? He grabbed the rope. After Leaning Tower he was broke. Caught stealing food from the Yosemite supermarket, he was jailed and deported. He escaped his escorts in Oregon and was back in Yosemite a few days later.

The long trip back came too soon. My last Valley season with Brian ended anticlimactically, driving homeward through summer rain, listening to cassette tapes of Jackson Browne. I climbed no more with Brian, but as I got older I turned to him several times for advice about life and once even a place to stay. He was one of the most generous, helpful and patient people I knew, and certainly the only climber in my immediate circle who had a successful career outside of climbing.

The last climbing trip of the year was to Weir, in Quebec. Judy sat beside Reg in the darkness so his hotfooting along the curving back roads wouldn't make her carsick. Sig and I were in the back seat. A plague of frogs covered the road, and at first Judy was horrified and winced at the increasing tempo of dull thuds of crushed frogs. Reg, who often swerved to flatten roadkill, was laughing with the rest of us at the unavoidable carnage, and soon Judy, despite being a committed vegetarian and animal lover, was laughing just as uncontrollably.

Reg took the single Murphy bed in our small roadside motel room, and Judy, Steve Labelle, Dave Lanman, Dave's girlfriend, Sig Isaac and me slept on the floor. Just as I fell asleep, Dave and his girlfriend started loudly making love. Steve got up in his underwear and kicked them until they stopped. "You can't behave like this," he said, "there are people here."

Water poured down the face the next day, after Dave and I had rappelled from near the top of Black and White, a monumental corner splitting an obsidian face near Weir. The storm caught us unprepared, turning our pant legs into drainpipes and giving us goosebumps as the carabiners squeezed black water onto our hands. At the bottom, Dave played a flake of rock with wired nuts as if it was a gong, singing one of his favourite Stones songs, grimacing at the rain and sucking on a cigarette.

Judy's rooming house for her first year at McGill was on the Avenue des Pins. It almost seemed to hang between the forests of Mount Royal and the apartments of the lower mountain. Thirty years later, I happened upon it again, out on a run during a visit to one of my daughters at McGill.

The Italianate leaves and flowers of the doorway reminded me of the little classical fountain in the foyer of Judy's father's house, and other parts reminded me of Judy herself. Boarded windows added to its drama, as if asking me to judge whether or not it should be demolished.

I remembered her at the window, naked to the waist, brown hair on white shoulders, cold blue eyes splintered with emerald, the river flowing towards the Atlantic, the smell of the stones and forest of Val-David still with us. We ate sandwiches and read a Spanish poem; the dog when the mistress is gone, the hidden treasures, the dampened pain. Memory has made her the paragon and conqueror of those years that completed her, but left me a wanderer.

Dave was living in Montreal at the time, in the basement of the frat house of Geoff Creighton, who we had met in the Gunks. Geoff and his partner Charlie Roberton were good rock climbers and obsessed ice climbers. Once, they hitch-hiked from Montreal to Banff to ice climb, winter camping on the way. They were also the only young climbers we had ever met who wanted to climb real mountains. Eventually Reg convinced Geoff to come to Ontario to devote himself to rock climbing at a safe distance from the mountains, but despite our efforts, Geoff become an amazing alpinist and climbed hard new routes in places like the Andes and the Saint Elias Range in the Yukon.

Dave had newspaper clippings about George Manson's

death, illustrated with photos of the Cassin Ridge. Geoff seemed like one of us when we went cragging, but when he commented intelligently about the conditions and nature of the route on that huge frozen face, his cosmopolitan alpine argot really impressed me. More so when, in '81, I heard that he and Dave Nettle, a climber from California, had climbed the Cassin Ridge via the same valley where George and his party had died.

On my last evening in Montreal, Dave and his girlfriend broke up, and he got drunk. The rumour that another climber rushed to console her was easy to believe. I soon left Dave's life for several years, ending a chapter in our friendship that had been formative for me.

He did, however, leave us something to remember him by. On the way home, we were pulled over by the Sûreté du Québec, who searched the car while Pete Reilly looked for food in the garbage can of a poutine stand. Pete found some fries, but the cops didn't find a bag of marijuana Dave had once lost in the car. It showed up under the driver's seat a year later, having twice crossed the US border.

Sig, Reg, Pete and me spent much of the last months of 1980 lifting weights, running miles of slushy sidewalks and reading climbing magazines. Reg and Sig Isaac taught themselves how to ice climb, but it was a warm winter. Perhaps the poor conditions and soft, thin ice laid the foundation for Reg's eventual aptitude for ice climbing. We chose Bancroft, the main ice-climbing area mentioned in the Ontario climbing guidebook at the time, to introduce Pete to ice climbing. When we arrived, all we found was bare rock and piles of splintered icicles. We got back in the car and drove to Rattlesnake.

On the way, we discussed Pete's new, short-lived plan to become a policeman. He had a copy of the personality tests and was worried about how to answer the questions. The first question was, "Have you ever stolen anything?" That was easy. After that, the intentions of the examiners were murkier. We speculated as to why they wanted to know if Pete had enjoyed books about imaginary worlds as a child.

Arriving as the light dimmed behind a wall of fog, we parked on a road below the cliff, scrambled to a ledge and unrolled our sleeping bags. We ate plastic-packaged Jos. Louis cakes for dinner, and Reg dropped a match on my nylon jacket while lighting a stove but patted it out. The scorched hole leaked feathers.

Pete balanced on a ledge, hands out like a wrestler's. "Spidey-senses on," he said, jumping through the mist to a thin maple.

Reg threw down an empty can when Pete told him to try the leap for himself. Pete called him a litterbug and pitched the can back up.

In the night, rangers shone lights up at the ledge. We lay still, giggling quietly until they left. It was still dark when I was woken by the sound of shattering glass. Down the cliffside, a bonfire of picnic tables and trees sent sparks up the wall. The red firelight made the revellers look like devils.

In the morning, the cliff streamed with water. Ashes hissed in the drizzle below the scorched overhang that became known as the Fireplace Wall. On the way out, rangers asked us if we had seen anyone camping on the rocks. Four miles away, on the slopes of Mount Nemo, they had seen a fire on the cliff.

A few days before New Year's, 1980, the mercury hovered at the freezing point. Sig, Reg and I drove snowy roads above Hamilton to Spencer Gorge, a sickle-shaped slit cut by a river into the mesa overlooking Dundas and Hamilton. There were lookouts where you could see orange flames in the steel-plant chimneys to the south. At one end of the gorge was Webster's Falls, which froze into a popular ice climb; at the other end, Tews Falls trickled off a high cliff. We came to climb the ice smearing the slopes between these waterfalls.

A steep step led to a 70-foot ice smear below a dripping icicle the diameter of a jet fuselage. We took off our jackets, donned crampons and descended unroped on ice softening in the warming air. As I looked into the kaleidoscope of the icicle, the tempo of its echoing drips seemed to quicken.

I climbed down past Sig, and then Reg, 50 feet below him. Near the bottom, I heard a loud crack, and chunks of ice struck my head and hands. I stepped off the ice smear to a ledge just as a torrent of ice flowed over me. When it ceased,

I looked up. The icicle had fallen and shattered, sweeping the icefall with debris. Thirty feet above me was Reg, bleeding from his head onto the ice.

In the shadows below, Sig had come to rest after a hundred-foot tumble. I tiptoed through the wreckage of the icicle, afraid I was approaching a corpse. Suddenly, he opened his eyes, jabbered and tried to crawl through the bloody snow. Covering him with my jacket, I tried to keep him still.

Reg made it down, although red stains were spreading on his toque and a pant leg slashed by Sig's crampons. I was uninjured, but if Reg stayed and I went for help, they might both go into shock. I stuffed a mitten under Reg's toque and he climbed out. Sig kicked as I fought to keep him out of the creek.

An hour later, the local firemen arrived and put Sig in a basket stretcher. A little portly but still capable, they stumbled up the hill in their rubber boots, manhandling Sig to the rim. An article in a local paper reported that a fireman had heart palpitations while rescuing us. Some climbers have had to live with the guilt caused by the death or injury of their rescuers, but luckily for the fireman and us, he survived and decided to retire.

At the hospital, a doctor bandaged Reg's head while he explained that Sig, who was retching in the next room from a morphine injection, needed many stitches, casts and tests. On the phone, I told my mother that everyone was sort of fine. I remembered how Chas Yonge had joked about what he would say in a post-mortem phone call to the parents of John Kaandorp, the hard-climbing kid from Hamilton who climbed with the rope tied in bowline around his waist. She was quiet and didn't even remind me that my father's dinner was at 5:30. As an adult, it's easy to imagine the stress my climbing sometimes caused my parents, but back then I never worried about it.

After ten days, Sig was moved from intensive care to a small hospital, and Reg convinced me to come with him to visit his Katimavik friends in Niagara Falls before we picked Sig up. On the way, we would find some ice rumoured to be near the hydroelectric plant. It was warm, however, and all we found was a narrow, hollow sheet of ice above a concrete turbine house. From the top, we could see our ice-axe picks sticking through the back of the ice. It began to rain and we gave up on climbing for the day. A security guard stopped his jeep and asked if we had seen any climbers. There had been a report. We said no, and he drove away.

Reg's friends served us a dinner of canned tomatoes at a folding card table. The can had been contaminated with large white grubs, which our hosts ate as if they were a normal accompaniment. Everyone was so drunk or drugged that I began to feel slow-moving and dull even though I hadn't had a drink.

Until recently, Niagara Falls had been a minor boom

town. There had been weddings, tourists, the year-long carnival of Clifton Hill and the bars full of kids coming to Canada from New York State for the lower drinking age. But since the drinking age was raised in Ontario, the wax museums, fun houses and bars had begun to close down. The honeymoon hotels were also laying people off. It was no wonder. "Who gets married these days?" one of our hosts asked.

Our hosts were going to jump their rent. Their backpacks were ready. It wasn't hopeless everywhere. They were going to Alberta, where they said an oil boom was creating a shortage of unskilled labour. They had been told that the West offered not only jobs but sunshine, wilderness, communes, cool people and dope, although they didn't actually seem to know anyone out there. On the way home, Reg talked even more about going west than he usually did, continuing even when high winds spun the car out of control on the snow-slick bridge over Hamilton harbour.

Reg signed Sig's discharge papers on a clipboard held by a nun who frowned at us, perhaps because she'd found the pornographic magazines we had sent him. We crammed Sig's cast-hobbled body into the back seat like a mannequin and brought him to Toronto. My mother felt sorry for him and let us keep him at our house for a couple of days, like he was a stray.

Sig told my mother he was born in Germany, his father was Mauritian and his mother lived in the Maritimes. At first, my mother clicked her tongue. Being abandoned by his mother made Sig a sympathetic character. She changed her mind when Sig's mother showed up on the doorstep a few days later. She had found out about the accident from his sister and rushed to Toronto.

Sig's mother took him to his sister's apartment in Don Mills. The glow of the television in the next room flickered on his wall and the freeway droned outside as he lay staring at the ceiling, unable even to get to the bathroom without help. Pete, Reg and I brought him cola and pencilled the number of pull-ups we did on the closet doorjamb on the wall.

While he healed, the American hostages held in Iran for 14 months were freed, BASE jumping was invented, Canadian gasoline pumps changed from gallons to litres, Reg worked as a fry cook at the Big Doughnut in Mimico and I sat, nearly uselessly, through school. Later, Sig said that the pain and the boredom were so overwhelming that if he had been able to get to the window, he would have thrown himself out. When spring came, the doctors cut off his casts and he rose from his bed. Against reason and our expectations, that winter had made us all braver and more serious, as though we had passed some kind of test.

At SEE's new industrial park digs, in the spring of 1981, at the age of 18, I ended almost a decade and a half of public school in a smattering of mediocre, half-hearted tests and papers for courses for the now-extinct Grade 13. SEE had changed. There was no graffiti and no student lounge. Gone were Laura Nyro, Nick Drake, the girls with elf names and the pot smokers dreaming about becoming jazz critics, public radio hosts or social workers. They had been replaced by Kyles and Jasons with the anarchy symbol daubed on their jackets in correction fluid. They bragged about joining the army or becoming pornographers. Like me, the punk rockers were at SEE just because they were lazy or didn't fit in, but I missed the self-conscious specialness of the old crowd. I was in a jaded mood that winter and ignored books to run in the snow, do pull-ups and wash dishes at a downtown restaurant.

That spring, Pete and Sig climbed the Zodiac on El Capitan, which was still considered difficult. The three-day climb up an overhanging wall was a big step for kids who had been climbing in deck shoes a couple of years before. There would be no big walls for me that summer. The money I made setting up top-ropes and washing dishes was spent on trips to the closer cliffs of New York and New Hampshire, where I climbed with whoever I could and lived off of macaroni and peanut butter.

Judy took summer courses at the state college in New Paltz but was back in Toronto on a visit when I was in the Gunks. At the Uberfall, I met a fellow with stringy hair and round, wire-rimmed glasses. He climbed at an easy grade and was looking for a partner. He could tell from my accent I was from Canada. His girlfriend was from Canada.

"Her name's Judy," he said. "She climbs at someplace called Rattlesnake Point. You ever been there?"

In September 1981 Judy and I sat across from each other in her parents' living room. Her hair was in a long braid, her skin white above the neckline of her blouse. The fountain in the foyer gurgled in the background. I had never been in the living room before, and it had the sterile feeling of a space reserved for important things.

Judy knew I had met him. She said I was always somewhere else, doing something different than her. She even thought about me when she was with him. But then she realized that was wrong. There was no need to discuss differences in our beliefs, I wouldn't understand the real reason it was happening this way: karma.

It seemed impossible that mere words could undo the memories of holding her, the storm at Bon Echo, the unrepeatable things she had said, her and Bea dancing in the aisle in tendrils of cannabis smoke. *"It's astounding, time is fleeting..."*

I said he didn't climb as well as me. Neither had I, she said, when we met and she first liked me. She looked into my eyes, hurt and confident. She wasn't indifferent; she was trying to find a way to part as equals. I could never see myself as her equal, but I succumbed.

I had no choice. When I told her I knew a girl who understood me better, she seemed not to care. I was no longer her concern.

I had no idea whether or not I was telling the truth about

being understood, but I had met a girl who liked climbing, and like me had nothing better to do. The same evening I told that girl that Sig, my brother and I were going west. We weren't coming back. She could come too.

CHAPTER 11

Eastern Bums and Creeps

Passage home? Never.
—HOMER, *The Odyssey*, 5.193

On an early fall morning in 1981, we put our climbing and camping gear into Reg's car to head west. I had packed the last of my childhood things – comic books, a cap pistol, some plastic models, an army helmet we had stolen from the depot by the bridge – in cardboard boxes and left them beneath the basement stairs with my concrete dumbbells. I forget what my mother was planning to do with my room. What couldn't fit in the trunk went on Gerry Banning's roof rack, which we took because it was still on Reg's car from an earlier trip, along with Gerry's camping stove and a pair of his climbing shoes. Gerry later wrote us a few hurt letters. He missed us, he said, even though we had stolen his stuff.

My father had begun to read about climbing, beginning, characteristically, with Victorian mountaineering books, which suggested to him that his sons had it all wrong. I appreciated that he was trying, though. Before I left, he gave me a copy of *Scrambles Amongst the Alps*, by Edward Whymper, who first climbed the Matterhorn. I put the book in my pack and I still have it.

My mother hugged Reg and me and gave us polyester fleece jackets she had sewn as farewell presents. A few days before, she had told me about forgoing an opportunity to be a missionary in the Arctic in order to marry my father. Perhaps the subtopian world they had built together for themselves and their children proved the rightness of her decision. Her damp eyes were a clue to a truth that I only realized years later: our lives weren't like those of the depressed characters in the mean-spirited and one-dimensional movies about the suburbs that were then becoming popular. My parents were good people who had tried to make the best choices for their family. I, however, knew that I did not belong in their world, and lacking any real mission, simply trusted that my own place could be reached in Reg's car.

When we pulled out of the driveway, I was thinking of local climbers who had gone west. Pete Arbic from Kingston had given up on the land and headed west. He financed himself by selling cheap climbing gear from Terry's basement store out of the back of his truck, spending a season in Boulder and Yosemite and eventually working in the same ski resort as Rob Rohn.

Other stories were about people I only knew by reputation. There was a climber who had run off with someone else's wife and made an early ascent of El Capitan. Another had gone to climb and became a dentist. There were others, but none of them were friends. I had no idea which provinces, cities or even mountain ranges any of them were in. The only people I would know when I got there were in the car with me. All I knew about where I was going was that there were places to climb, mountains and jobs.

A day later, we wound our way along the north shore of Lake Superior, where the hills were turning yellow and red. On the second night, we slept on the prairie. On the third day, we drove through Calgary. We planned to return to the city to work, but first we hoped to climb a little in the Rockies to the west.

Banff was rainy. The only glimpse we got of the peaks was on postcards and in snow globes in gift shops. We hoped to find information about rock climbs in an outdoor store. By a stone fireplace decorated with crossed ice axes, we looked through the guidebook to Yamnuska, a thousand-foot limestone wall near Canmore. I recognized the name of Urs Kallen, the author, from the first-ascent credits in the Bon Echo chapter of the Ontario climbing guidebooks.

A salesman with long hair, a new fleece jacket and a Tibetan scarf asked if he could help us. It was Henry, from the surplus sports store in Toronto. When I reminded him that we had both ice climbed with Brian Hibbert, he said they weren't hiring and that the cheap camping was at Tunnel Mountain. There were more jobs in Calgary, he said. I bought Urs Kallen's Yamnuska guidebook at a counter displaying a stack of felt hats with edelweiss brooches.

An hour later, we parked by the white chateau of Lake Louise. Across the cold turquoise of the lake, the wind shredded the clouds, revealing the white glaciers and grey walls of the Rockies. Little rowboats on the lake made it look like a scene from a painting I had seen as a child. We would be back in winter to climb on waterfalls beside the footpaths with ice axes and crampons, but we knew nothing about how to climb mountains like these.

The peaks we had chosen were the Bugaboos, mainly because the guidebook dust jacket had a photo of the granite tooth of Pigeon Spire poking out of a glacier on the cover. It looked like Yosemite, apart from the glaciers, which we saw as unimportant, despite the obvious dangers and challenges they presented to knowledgeable mountaineers. We were emboldened by the knowledge that some Bugaboo walls, including the difficult South Face of Snowpatch Spire, had been free climbed by Rob and Tom, who, like us, had climbed at Rattlesnake Point. Unlike us, however, they knew how to read the weather, rescue someone who fell in a glacier crevasse and avoid rockfall.

Rattling down the road from Brisco to the Bugaboos took two hours, which I spent looking at the guidebook. The authors used fewer words to describe a thousand feet of climbing than Jim Mark used for a few hundred. The book covered scores of mountains spread over thousands of square miles. Its language was archaic, with words like *athwart* for climbing on a ridge and *gnarly* as a description of texture. The road ended at a clearing. Above, the flow of the blue glaciers was divided by the stone pyramids of the Bugaboo Group. It was obvious why they had become the most famous rock-climbing peaks in the Purcell Range. A three-mile trail led up beside the tongue of a glacier to a military-looking Quonset already deserted for the season by the ranger. It was set among rocks, close to the foot of the Crescent Glacier, a milky eye of ice ringed by vertical spires.

Reg and Sig planned to do a five-hundred-foot climb on Crescent Spire called McTech Arête. All they knew about it was what someone had told them in the climbing store in the Gunks. It was a crack on a ridge said to be impossible to miss. There were many variations on the ridge, including a very hard one by Hugh, the young Gunks expert, but they were sure they could stay on route simply by climbing the easiest looking cracks.

I chose an easier but longer climb for my girlfriend and

me: the east ridge of Bugaboo Spire. It was a thousand-foot-long buttress seamed with perfect cracks. It had been first climbed in 1958 by three Princeton students and the enigmatic John Turner.

We started out before dawn on the moonlit glacier, our sneakers crunching on the cold snow. Near the gun-sight shoulder between the massive hulks of Bugaboo and Crescent spires, we heard a stream coursing through a crevasse. Icicles drooled from its edges. Crevasses were sometimes hidden by a crust of snow thin enough to be pierced by a footstep. Even for real mountaineers, who roped up and knew how to pull each other out, falling into a crevasse was serious. Not knowing how to rope up properly, we had simply not bothered.

At the foot of the peak, we climbed down a steep wall of snow, digging frozen fingers into the ice and jumping a gap between the mountain and the glacier. Four or five rope-lengths of easy scrambling led to the ridge. From there, it was a safe and interesting climb on compact granite to the top of the ridge. We ate snow and moved quickly, trying not to think about our hunger and thirst. Rappelling the route would have required leaving behind more equipment than we had brought, so we crossed the icy summit ridge to descend the lower-angled Kain Route. We wanted to sign the summit register, but it was fused shut by lightning. From the summit, Snowpatch Spire seemed a stone's throw away.

The summit was undercut by an overhanging wall called

the Gendarme. Austrian-Canadian guide Conrad Kain, after whom both the hut and the first route up the mountain were named, climbed the Gendarme on the first ascent in 1916. At the same time, my ancestors were fighting his former countrymen in France. Kain's work guiding clients up the hardest and highest peaks in the Rockies without much safety equipment paid better than the Western Front but wasn't much safer.

We rappelled down a few short walls, kicked steps across snowy ledges in our rubber-soled roc k shoes and picked our way down rock bands to the snow slope between Bugaboo and Snowpatch spires. As darkness rose, the air cooled and we made smaller and smaller steps with our heels as the snow hardened. When it finally froze, we slid to the glacier on our backsides. We looked up at the vertical east face of Bugaboo Spire, listening to the trickle and bounce of falling rock. The next season, a climber was crushed by rockfall where we stood.

The hut was shadowed by the spires when we arrived, although distant ranges still glowed red. Reg and Sig were already inside. Sig's arm was crudely bandaged. I was exhausted and dehydrated and so used to seeing Sig in casts or bandages that it took a few seconds before I realized that there had been an accident.

A man with slick black hair rifled a first-aid kit nailed to the wall. He was wiry and short like Joe Bones and had penetrating eyes, but his disintegrating pile jacket made him look like a beggar. His face was fleshless and his complexion white as a vampire's. His long mouth curled into a smile with a couple of twists he wasn't born with. In a thick Irish accent, Preston explained that Reg and Sig had had "a bit of an aggro" with loose rock, but there were no painkillers.

Sig was in a solitary confinement crouch in the corner, staring at the floor and holding his arm. Reg ate from a bag of instant Chinese noodles. They had climbed five pitches, but the summit had still been still hundreds of feet of lower-angled climbing above. So they'd decided to solo to the top, as if they had been at Rattlesnake Point. Just below the summit, Reg knocked off a stone that could have sent Sig to his death but luckily just gashed his arm.

Preston made a darning gesture, curled his upper lip and offered to stitch it up, a trick he claimed to have picked up in the army. Sig just stared. Preston pointed at our frozen rock shoes and the trainers still dangling from our harnesses and laughed. He listed our mistakes: no ice axes, no mountaineering boots for the approach and descent, only one rope, no crevasse rescue gear, no headlamps, no water or extra clothes. Since we had gotten away with it, I rankled a little, but it made me realize how close we had come to being stuck on the mountain, sucked into a crevasse, crushed by rockfall or sent sliding to our deaths. I went to sleep thinking about how lucky we had been.

Rain pelting the corrugated walls woke us at mid-morning. It wasn't the first time Preston had been trapped in a hut in bad weather, and he whiled away some of the time with his story. He had grown up Protestant on a Catholic street in Ulster. By the time he was a teenager, he was already a street fighter. As soon as he was old enough, he joined the army. The army taught him to climb, and when he went back to civilian life, he became the total 1970s climber, right out of the pages of *Mountain* magazine. He went on expeditions to the Himalayas and the Andes and climbed many of the notable faces in the Alps. In the Lake District of northern England, where he had briefly been a postman, he climbed every route in the thick guidebook.

Preston's girlfriend, Eileen, was a quiet schoolteacher from the south of Ireland. They had just come from Yosemite and were heading to Calgary. Preston had British climbing friends who had been hired illegally by Calgary contractors scrambling to meet the demand for new construction. He hoped to get similar work and save enough money to climb for months in California in the spring. On our third day in the Bugaboos, rain became snow and we squelched down the path to the car. Preston and Eileen stayed in the hut to wait out the weather. We would meet them again soon.

We drove the car north to a gas station at the intersection with the Trans-Canada Highway. We finally figured out that our watches were two hours ahead of the local time. We had adjusted them by an hour in Winnipeg and assumed that this put us in the time zone for the rest of the country. Our mistake might have saved us grief. Starting earlier than we thought in the Bugaboos meant having more time to make our approaches in the morning and having as much light as possible for the steeper, harder sections. Even with the extra-early start we had finished our climb in the dark.

Losing two hours made us all feel sleepy and disoriented. We traded places in the driver's seat frequently as we twisted our way westwards through the river canyons shared by the railway. It was dotted with place names that reminded me of studying the railway in grade school: Kootenay, Yoho, Kamloops. We stopped for dinner in Chilliwack, which we only knew as the name of a rock band. It was hot and dry and the locals eyed us suspiciously at a gas station.

A day later we drove along the Pacific coast to a bench above Howe Sound. In the distance were snow-capped mountains. Below us, Squamish lay under the paper mill's invisible, foul-smelling sulphur cloud. Above the highway soared the 1,500-foot wall of Squamish Chief.

The next morning we gathered our equipment and found the trailhead by the relief of a climber carved on a low rock. Furry green moss flowed down granite boulders and trees that spread like tentacles towards the forest floor. Above rose the Grand Wall, a climb first done in 1961 by Ed Cooper and

Jim Baldwin. The striking black-and-white photos Cooper later took appeared in many climbing books. In 1961 he and Baldwin had been teenagers looking for a summer climbing project. Their climb made them local celebrities. On weekends, the road below the Chief had been jammed with cars full of rubberneckers. The climbers camped in a ruined shack below the wall, dated local girls and received gifts of food and equipment from townspeople.

It was a weekday, and although there were now many routes up the wall, and British Columbia climbers who were world experts on big-wall climbing practiced there, we had the wall to ourselves.

After a couple of pitches in a corner, the wall steepened. We used webbing slings to climb a line of bolts up a slab to a one-hundred-foot candle of stone called the Split Pillar. I climbed up the crack's right side, but after 20 feet my arms gave out. Anders Ourom's new guidebook gave it a grade I had climbed often, but we pulled up on nuts and pitons, even in places where Ourom gave moderate, free-climbing grades. After that, I never understood why people said the grades at Squamish were easy.

I was exhausted, penniless, homeless, unemployed, three thousand miles from home, halfway up a wall, hanging from a rusty bolt, wondering whether I was just afraid or my technique was poor, but I was having fun. Fortunately, the crack soon eased a little and the rest of wall had many bolts and fixed pitons. By late afternoon, we reached a damp and mossy ledge leading to the forest.

In the morning we washed in a frigid stream flowing from the mountains and turned the car eastwards. Sig would later wonder why we hadn't just stayed in Vancouver, with its excellent rock, friendly climbing community and enticing hippie neighbourhoods. In fact, it would have been harder than returning to Alberta. Rent in Vancouver was higher than in Calgary, and jobs were as scarce as they were at home. Sig, however, moved to Vancouver in the late 1980s and set records for speed climbing some of Squamish's hard routes.

Although we were almost broke, we decided to eke out a visit to one last cliff before looking for work in Calgary. After another long day in the car, we were back in the eastern hills of the Rockies, below the rock wall of Yamnuska for our final climb of the year.

When my SEE schoolmate Brandy Greenwood's father, Brian, arrived in Calgary from England, there were only two climbs at Yamnuska. It was easy to see why as I looked up at its smooth grey faces and yellow towers of loose rock. Brian Greenwood, however, wasn't scared and added many more routes, naming some after the demons of Middle-earth – Smeagol, Gollum, Balrog. The names of its heroes were reserved for his children.

Reg and I took turns leading. It wasn't difficult when the grey limestone was rough and gave great holds for our boots, but the yellow cracks, with their caches of loose rock, were frightening. From Redshirt you could see vertical fields of steep, unexplored rock. In the decade ahead, these faces would be visited by young climbers who took huge falls, crushed each other with rocks and then sawed off their own plaster casts to get back on the cliffs. One of them died after a fall. Steve De Maio from Burlington was used to ground-grazing falls at Mount Nemo when he joined them. "If you think Yamnuska is loose," he said, "wait until you get to Mount Nemo." I understood what he meant, but although Nemo and Yamnuska were both loose, Yamnuska was ten times as high.

It irked me that the locals thought of Yamnuska as a crag when it had so much in common with an alpine face. The only loose rock I had climbed before Yamnuska was relatively close to the ground in stable weather. Yosemite was high, but the weather and the rock were excellent. I had done a few climbs on which it was hard to figure out which way the route went, or I had to set up difficult belays, but I had never had to avoid rockfall. In fact, I didn't even own a climbing helmet. I had never climbed while wearing a pack, which I would have to do if I wanted to bring extra clothes in case of bad weather.

Back home, mountaineering was an expensive and romantic pastime for the well-off, because mountains were so far away. Ontario mountaineers saw rock climbing as practice for mountains, and getting good at practicing just didn't make sense. At Yamnuska, rock climbing and mountaineering were obviously part of the same continuum. It wasn't a surprise, therefore, that many of the Albertan climbers we met rock climbed for kicks and grades but thought alpine routes were the ultimate prizes.

The Mountain Equipment Co-op store was the first place we went in Calgary, simply because we knew there would be climbers there. The long rack of ice axes and hammers, mountain-climbing boots, climbing hardware and ski-mountaineering equipment I had only seen in photos reinforced the impression I had gotten at Yamnuska that mountaineering was as normal here as street racing was in Etobicoke. The guys behind the counter, however, were young climbers like us and helped us out by telling us someone was renting out an apartment close by.

The superintendent opened his door slowly and stood there in his briefs, heavy metal blaring from his stereo. He asked if we were Easterners, told us not to party or make noise and said we could have the apartment if we paid first and last month's rent in cash, which left us with about $20. We spent the two days before the place was available sleeping by the quartzite boulders at Big Rock near Okotoks and looking for work.

Money flowing from the oil sands created unskilled jobs that paid well and attracted what Calgary's hard-drinking mayor called "eastern bums and creeps." The mayor offered to pay their bus fare back whence they came, but their very presence was a measure of the city's ascendancy.

At night vagrants from rodeo towns and eastern cities staggered through the streets, hammered on drugs and alcohol. Maritimers drank jovially or spilled brawling into the street. There were streets where dozens of prostitutes loitered at night. Girls from Quebec sat in hippie tea rooms listening to sitar music and studying English before punching in for shifts at luxury hotels filled with Texans and Saudis. German sedans idled outside restaurants where Frederic Remington replicas were being hung as mining speculators drank single-malt whisky and ate their first $50 steaks.

A few days after we arrived, Sig, four Vietnamese-Canadians and I were given brown polyester uniforms and jobs in the wine cellar of a downtown hotel. My first duty was building a tower of champagne bottles for a reception celebrating a merger of two oil exploration companies. A man with a cavalry sabre tried to cut the top off a bottle but stumbled, triggering an avalanche of bottles that smashed and foamed on the floor. We picked him up, towelled off his suit and dusted his Stetson, and the party continued. The Swiss sommelier said he could smell the wine's distinctive aromas as we wrung it out of dishcloths into a plastic bucket.

Reg's cooking training got him a job in a bistro. Despite high prices and a full house every night, there were weeks when the owners' renovation and cocaine bills left no money to pay him. Reg resorted to the ancient form of wage recovery and stole food and wine.

A boutique climbing store gave Reg a day job and a more reliable paycheque. Patrons tried on the newest technology – waterproof, breathable jackets – as Reg stood with the other colour options draped over his forearm. He helped them select an ice axe just barely long enough to graze the palm while the ferrule touched the floor, although he himself had never used one.

He heard gossip about who would go on the upcoming Canadian Mount Everest expedition. There was tension between some experienced expat Brits and talented, young, Canadian-born climbers. Leadership of the expedition had changed hands several times. It was exciting to hear about, even if you were strictly a rock climber. Mount Everest had only been climbed by a handful of top mountaineers, and guided commercial ascents of the mountain were unthinkable. Although Italian Reinhold Messner had just climbed Everest alone and without supplemental oxygen, major Himalayan expeditions were still large and named after the nationality of the climbers, partly to elicit patriotic donations.

Reg heard about a mountain club that met once a week. We were a little apprehensive as we descended through layers of cigarette smoke to the ersatz English pub where they met. Most of the climbers in the basement bar wore fleece jackets and had beards and long hair. They looked like they had come from the pages of *Hard Rock,* and some of them had. That night I heard the names of many of the world's climbing areas pronounced in half a dozen British dialects. It was easy to see why visiting British climbers often said the club made them feel like they were back home.

They didn't have Kahlúa, the only alcoholic beverage Sig drank, so he ordered a cola. Reg and I asked for beer, and some Brits smirked while I was carded.

Preston's British expat friends got him and Eileen a room in a dilapidated house in the rough neighbourhood by the old Stampede grounds. A silent man said to be one of the world's leading cavers lived in the unfurnished basement. Preston, the caver and two huge Brits who were obviously brothers arrived together, sat down with us and launched into a discussion about collecting garbage in Chamonix, getting drunk in Wales, getting drunker in Germany, a route they had tried in the Andes and whether tourists or sailors made better mugging victims. A little awestruck and too broke for a second beer, we went back to the apartment. Preston and the caver, who, I learned, couldn't drink or speak because his jaw had been wired shut after a bar fight, stumbled a few steps behind.

A little group on the apartment floor drank warm white wine from plastic cups. A short-haired female backpacker from New Zealand sat with the climbers we had met at the co-op. Sig reclined against a blank tombstone he had brought home, as if he was reserving it for his own use. The impression was strengthened by his stack of paperbacks by Albert Camus, Jean-Paul Sartre, Louis-Ferdinand Céline, Leonard Cohen and Henry Miller. Like the characters in these books, Sig started treating the world's pleasures as distractions and its rewards as illusions. Unlike them, he believed the world offered total compensation for these inadequacies through climbing.

Preston, who was slurring his words, said something about the Everest expedition that started an argument with the local climbers. I ignored them and sipped the stolen wine. I silently marvelled about how I had come from a scrap of shale on the other side of the continent to a room where a fight might break out about Mount Everest.

The next morning Reg and I staggered to his car in the parking lot below. This piece of junk – originating in an underpass scrapyard by Six Points Plaza, and now about to take us to the walls of the Ghost River – felt more like home than the apartment.

The potholes on the road into the Ghost loosened the dashboard, and the glovebox door fell off. I was relieved when Reg finally said we were in the right place. We didn't have a guidebook, but he said our climb was nearby – coincidentally close to the spot where he had finally decided the car could take no more.

The customer at the shop who had told him about the climb had said to bring pitons. Reg only had one pin and neither of us had a hammer, so he dropped a hand-sized stone into his chalk bag. I played out the belay rope as he climbed up the angle of stone to a grey overhang. There, the rock hammer disintegrated in his hand and the piton sprung from a crack and pinged off the scree before scything through the trees. We both laughed until he shouted and pointed to the distance, where a wild sheep bounced down a chimney twice as high as Bon Echo. Every leap and hoof-skittering landing made it look like the animal would careen to a bloody end on the talus, but it didn't. Safe on the ground, it rested for a moment before disappearing unharmed into the forest.

CHAPTER 12

Tell Him I Haven't Changed

T he phone rang early the next morning. Judy was calling from New Paltz to wish me a happy 19th birthday. I
was drowsy, and her voice surprised me with the memory of
childhood birthdays and a faint current of the electricity of
being near her.

She had a favour to ask. Her boyfriend had crashed his
motorcycle and she had fallen from the pillion seat. Apart
from a few bruises, they were both fine. The incident had
worried her, but not because the motorcycle was dangerous.
She was calling to ask me not to tell anyone who might tell
her parents that the boyfriend was sharing the apartment
her father rented for her. As my mind slowly returned to the
waking world, I said there was no need to worry; after all, a
continent lay between us.

She was getting ready to go to the University of California, she said. I was getting ready to go to work at the hotel kitchen. There was no way to make my job sound glamorous.

Over the next five years, she earned a graduate degree in computer science and began to teach courses and develop software for satellite imaging. During that time, I became a mediocre university student and a guidebook author, still immersed in climbing, intermittent with a long-term girlfriend, living in public housing. The rest of my life was still a question mark.

I met Judy again when she was visiting her family and dropped by Rattlesnake Point. She wasn't surprised to find me there.

I led her up some climbs and tried to show off. It wasn't easy; her partners in the Gunks had included some of the best climbers there. As we sat on a ledge during a brief shower that sent most of the climbers home, she asked if I wanted to see a photograph. It was of her in the door of the NASA Hercules in a tie-dye shirt. She kept it in her wallet in case she got pulled over by the cops. Someone told her they never ticket astronauts, she laughed.

She earned enough to split her time between the mountains of New England, where we had gone on our first climbing trip, and the California coast's hills and beaches. It was like a dream, she said, and I agreed.

At the end of the afternoon, we scrambled up the descent gully and over the clifftop, turning our backs on the cliff together for the last time. She was quiet for a few minutes and then said she had brought her birth control in case I was here. We could do it in the back of her car, which she had left in the old abandoned lot outside the park, also in case she met me.

When I had watched her in the window of the Avenue des Pins or been with her any number of places we might have made love, one of our gestures or circumstances stopped us. The first person that I knew she'd had made love to had been the fellow I met in the Gunks who asked me if I knew her.

I had learned how to lead up to the act and enjoyed the little competencies and flatteries that improved or hurt my chance of success when I finally took it. All that was excluded when she stopped my rough hands beneath her woollen sweater and struggled to get out of her jeans. Pullovers caught on our limbs in the narrow space, and we took off just enough for the act.

She closed her eyes, kissed me once and lay on her back. My face was in her chestnut hair, full of the smell of chalk, and I wanted to kiss her but she held me where I was. The odour of her sweat joined that of the chalk and a faint rumour of her sex as she wrapped her legs around, taking me into her. She had offered to fuck and now we were. I can't remember what it felt like to be in her or to come, but now the moment seems to complete the story of the young lovers.

Sitting on the rocks surrounding the empty parking lot

afterwards, she lit a joint. You shouldn't have to love someone to have sex with them. You could do it with friends, and we were friends, she said. Her hands were shaking.

The next time I heard anything about her was after my brother, Reg, met her at a party in the '90s. I have a message for David, she told him. Tell him I haven't changed.

Through a network of friends, I learned in the 2000s that she had been diagnosed with cancer. When the doctor told her not to climb anymore, she went to a park and hugged a boulder and said goodbye to rock climbing. She chose for her grave a little peninsula of stone where the westerly bowed a white pine over the cold, dark water. Before she died, she posted a photograph on her website that was taken in the Gunks when she was 17.

Her cheeks are high but round, her lips wide. She smiles, exposing teeth on which someone must have spent a lot of money. In the green Catskill forest light and the climbing clothes that were never made small enough to fit her, she looks fairy-like. She leans towards the diagonal black margin of the photo that elided me from that fall day when, as the Instamatic clicked, I had been close enough to share her breath.

I think of Akhmatova: "though you are three times more beautiful than angels, though you are a sister to the river willows." Though. Though you made love to me in the back of a car at Rattlesnake Point, now you dwell in the ether, and I in the unformed possibilities of mortal life. I sit by myself on the ledge where you said you would tell the cops you were an astronaut if they caught you speeding.

But the ledge is part of the stone that brought us together, gave life to our relationship and poisoned it too. I admit I loved it more than you.

Sometimes a vulture, the bird that wastes nothing, sits in its tattered black soutane watching me from an ancient grey stick twisting from the wall. His grandfather was there when, as a child on McGillivray's Hill, I poked my head over the cliff edge. I remember him circling around the fallen temple of the burned hilltop barn, and he was there when I grasped my first handhold as if I might shake all the world by it.

My companions and I came to know and name every crack and facet of the rocks as if they had been created for us alone. The names of most of us will barely be remembered in the histories of climbing, and ultimately the names we called the rocks will be forgotten.

Now the escarpment still whips its stone tail through the great blue lake, brown fields and scrubby green woodlots, past the vast cities and fiery steel plants, noble as a ship's bow here, blown to bits for driveway gravel and carved for church facades there; a garbage tip, ski slope, nursery for thousand-year-old trees and lookout. And, for a few lucky ones like me, it's something to climb.

Once I climbed it, I didn't much want to do anything else.

There have been days and even years when I have found that hard to defend. In such times I have told myself I will become a reverse Adam and un-call the names of the stones so that climbing will be no more for me. Then, I think, I could visit the cliffs and see only accidents of geology.

Yet, as the face's shadows mottle the talus and the water burbles in the spring, I realize that it isn't the cliffs but my life that would lack form if I gave up my history as a climber. This is the home and history I have always wanted. Equipment jangles as climbers on their first leads move tentatively upwards. Voices tremulous with fear or anticipation telling belayers to pay attention or to take up ropes reawaken the sense that the place still promises something for me to discover as well; something wonderful that's just a little more climbing away. And, because I am alive, I have the afternoon to waste finding it.

A Climbing Glossary

AID CLIMBING: Using equipment, whether pitons, bolts or nuts, to support your weight or to get higher. Not as esteemed as free climbing.

ALPINE CLUB OF CANADA (TORONTO SECTION): The national mountaineering club was founded in Winnipeg in 1906. The Toronto Section was founded in 1910 but died out by 1925 or so and revived in 1956, when climbing at Bon Echo began.

BELAY: To hold the rope to stop a falling climber. In the period described in this book, techniques progressed from passing the rope around the back for added friction, to tying hitches that locked the rope if the climber fell, to using simple devices like the Sticht plate. The place on a climb where one belays can also be referred to as the belay.

BIG WALL: A climb taking more than a day and requiring a bivouac.

CARABINER: A metal snap-link used in numerous climbing techniques.

CLEAN CLIMBING: Climbing using protection devices that can be placed and removed without a hammer. It was introduced to decrease the scarring of the rock caused by hammering pitons in and out.

CRUX: The most difficult section of a climb.

FIRST ASCENT / FIRST FREE ASCENT: The first ascent is the first time a climb is done by anyone. The first free ascent is the first time a climb previously done using aid is climbed without it. Both of these are more prestigious than repeating existing climbs.

FREE CLIMBING: Climbing using the natural features of the rock and deploying equipment only to catch a fall.

FREE SOLOING: Climbing without a rope.

LEADING: Climbing first and using protection attached to a rope with carabiners to make yourself safer. Leading is more dangerous and daring than following or top-roping.

NUT: A piece of metal with a wire or rope sling designed to be placed by hand in a crack and clipped to the rope with a carabiner to protect the lead climber in case of a fall. It is removed by hand by the second climber. Due to the range of crack sizes in a rock, a climber has to carry a selection of nuts.

PRUSIK: A hitch tied around a climbing rope with a sling that locks when weighted and can be loosened when weight is removed and slid up the rope. Used for crevasse rescue and occasionally for climbing a hanging rope.

RACK: A selection of protection devices, such as nuts and Friends, attached to a sling with carabiners and worn over the shoulder by the lead climber.

RAPPELLING: Descending a climb by fixing a rope to an anchor and sliding down it, using a technique or device to add friction to the rope and slow the descent. The rope is typically doubled through the anchors so that it can be pulled down when the rappellers reach the bottom.

SECOND: To climb after the lead climber, removing protection as you go. As safe as top-roping but usually done out of necessity to get the protection, rather than for its own sake.

SLING: A short length of webbing or cord tied or sewn into a loop. Slings have numerous uses in rock climbing.

TOP-ROPING: Setting up a rope from the top of a climb to avoid the risks of lead climbing.

Selected Books

Bonington, Chris. *Annapurna South Face*. London: Cassell, 1971.

———. *I Chose to Climb*. London: Gollancz, 1966.

Brown, Joe. *The Hard Years: An Autobiography*. London: Gollancz, 1967.

Godfrey, Bob, Dudley Chelton, and American Alpine Club. *Climb!* Boulder, CO: Alpine House, 1977.

Greenwood, B., and Urs Kallen. *A Climber's Guide to Yamnuska*. Calgary, AB: Brian Greenwood and Urs Kallen, 1970.

Jones, Chris. *Climbing in North America*. Berkeley: University of California Press, 1976.

Kruszyna, Robert, and William Lowell Putnam. *A Climber's Guide to the Interior Ranges of British Columbia – South*. New York: American Alpine Club, 1977.

Mark, James, Alpine Club of Canada, and Toronto Section of the Alpine Club of Canada. *A Guide to Rock Climbing in Ontario.* Scarborough, ON: Toronto Section of the Alpine Club of Canada, 1974.

Mark, James, Roger Parsons, Alpine Club of Canada, and Toronto Section of the Alpine Club of Canada. *Climbing in Southern Ontario.* Toronto: Toronto Section, Alpine Club of Canada, 1980.

Messner, Reinhold. *The Seventh Grade: Most Extreme Climbing.* New York: Oxford University Press, 1974.

Meyers, George. *Yosemite Climber.* Modesto, CA: Mountain Letters, 1979.

———. *Yosemite Climbs: Topographic Drawings of the Best Rockclimbing Routes in Yosemite Valley.* Modesto, CA: Mountain Letters, 1977.

Ourom, Anders, and British Columbia Mountaineering Club. *A Climber's Guide to the Squamish Chief.* Vancouver: B.C. Mountaineering Club, 1980.

Pearson, Mike, Ken Wilson, and Lucy Pearson. *Hard Rock: Great British Rock-Climbs.* London: Granada, 1974.

Poisson, Bernard. *Escalades: guide des parois, région de Montréal.* Montréal: Éditions la Cordée, 1971.

Rébuffat, Gaston. *Men and the Matterhorn*. New York: Oxford University Press, 1967.

———. *On Snow and Rock*. New York: Oxford University Press, 1963.

Rébuffat, Gaston, and Pierre Tairraz. *Between Heaven and Earth*. London: Kaye and Ward, 1970.

Robbins, Royal. *Advanced Rockcraft*. Glendale, CA: La Siesta Press, 1973.

———. *Basic Rockcraft*. Glendale, CA: Siesta Press, 1971.

Roper, Steve, and Allen Steck. *Fifty Classic Climbs of North America*. San Francisco: Sierra Club Books, 1979.

Rowell, Galen A. *The Vertical World of Yosemite: A Collection of Photographs and Writings on Rock Climbing in Yosemite*. Berkeley, CA: Wilderness Press, 1974.

Williams, Richard C. *Shawangunk Rock Climbs*. New York: American Alpine Club, 1972.

———. *Shawangunk Rock Climbs*. New York: American Alpine Club, 1980.